INDUSTRIAL DEMOCRACY
AND INDUSTRIAL MANAGEMENT

TECHNOLOGY AND DEMOCRATIC SOCIETY

An international series of publications concerned with relationship between the requirements of technology in work organizations and the needs, potentialities and aspirations of their members.

ERIC RHENMAN

INDUSTRIAL DEMOCRACY AND INDUSTRIAL MANAGEMENT

A CRITICAL ESSAY ON THE POSSIBLE MEANINGS AND IMPLICATIONS OF INDUSTRIAL DEMOCRACY

LONDON: TAVISTOCK

ASSEN: VAN GORCUM

First published in 1968
By Tavistock Publications Limited
11 New Fetter Lane, London E.C. 4
In association with Van Gorcum & Comp. N.V.
Printed in the Netherlands by Royal VanGorcum Ltd., Assen

I.I

SBN 422 73120 X

Translated from the Swedish by Mrs. Nancy Adler
Original version: Företagsdemokrati och företrgsorgonisation: P.A. Norstedt & Söners Förlag, Stockholm 1964.

Distributed in the U.S.A. by Barnes & Noble, Inc.

FOREWORD

In 1963 the Swedish Federation of Employers first approached the Business Research Institute at the Stockholm School of Economics about a program of research in the field of industrial democracy. The assignment was to include a survey of the relevant literature and an analysis of what it contained, thus providing a conceptual and theoretical frame-work for studying the problems that beset this whole subject. The report was first published in Swedish at the beginning of 1964.

What are the problems of industrial democracy? Can we resolve conflicts in company or labor market? If the company changes its decision structure, perhaps by introducing "Mitbestimmung", what will be the effects? Such questions and some possible answers are discussed in this volume. The main conclusions can be summarized as follows:

The industrial democracy debate has always been concerned with ends and means. Two goals in particular seem to recur in almost all the arguments: increasing productivity and the balancing of various interests in the company. The concept of productivity, however, must be redefined to include job satisfaction among the company's "products".

The main task facing researchers is to trace the relation between these goals and the various means. Where do we stand today? To take first the balance of interests and how it can be influenced, we can study the present machinery for conflict resolution in companies – machinery for which management is mainly responsible. The chief "stakeholders" in the company, whose interests will almost certainly clash, are the customers, the shareholders, and the employees. But the state, the local authorities and the suppliers too – to take a few examples – can at times be the source of pressing or awkward demands. To resolve this conflict several institutions are used, such as the market (commodity market, labor market), joint decision-making (e.g. negotiations) or co-optation (the stakeholders represented on management). One of the vital questions facing us today is: which institutions are compatible with the legitimate demands of the employees? We already have the labor market, with employer/trade union negotiations, we have works councils and consultation with the bosses. But is this enough? And if not, what else do we need? On the second count – increasing productivity through industrial democracy – we can look at what leadership research has to say. Unfortunately results show no clearcut connection between type of leadership and productivity. Rather, to achieve greater productivity, leadership style has to be adapted to the needs of the moment. What is more, our belief in the importance of leadership style for productivity and job satisfaction proves to have been greatly exaggerated. What *is* decisive is the whole technical and social situation.

Some practical conclusions can be drawn from this analysis: conditions can be improved. But there are no cast-iron solutions; measures and cures must be flexible. What can and must be improved, in fact, is business management itself, in the broadest sense of the term.

Works councils, participation in management and other schemes alone are not enough. Of far greater importance are such things as better planning, clearer company policies, improved management training and the adaption of wage systems and even the whole production system to the needs of the people concerned.

In editing the English version of this report I have tried to avoid reference to Scandinavian conditions. On the other hand my general frame of reference could but be influenced by my experience of the situation in Scandinavia, with its private enterprise, powerful unions, and extensive use of advisory councils.

The complete list of references from the original report has been reduced. Some references to works not available in English have been left out. I should like to mention three authors who have particularly influenced me, namely Chester Barnard, Herbert Simon and Philip Selznick.

Stockholm
September 1967 ERIC RHENMAN

CONTENTS

CHAPTER 1
INDUSTRIAL DEMOCRACY – RIPE FOR REAPPRAISAL

A. INTRODUCTION

SOME QUESTIONS OF TOPICAL INTEREST

Ever since the early days of industrialization the demand for fuller democracy in working life has been an important feature of many political programs. It has also been an object of intense interest to many employers and trade union leaders. But for the most part this demand has been expressed in rather vague terms. It seems that the whole subject is now ripe for further and more detailed discussion at any rate in those countries which already enjoy some measure of economic and political democracy.

We may wonder why industrial democracy is of such burning interest just now. A few of the possible reasons can be briefly mentioned.

The results of various experiments initiated by several countries in the rather special conditions of the Second World War and the immediate post-war period are now beginning to mature. Examples are readily found: England's wartime productivity councils, later replaced by various types of works councils; in Sweden the joint consultation committees agreed upon in 1946; the German Mitbestimmung, introduced into the steel and coal industries in 1951 and into other industries in a modified form in 1952; the Yugoslavian workers' councils set up in 1950; and various attempts to introduce profit-sharing in the United States, England and elsewhere.

In many Western countries it seems that the economic, political and social climate is now such that industrial democracy can be discussed responsibly by the parties concerned. Naturally this applies chiefly to countries, such as England and the Scandinavian nations, where negotiation rather than legislation has been the traditional method of solving industrial problems.

A third factor is certainly the present intense search for new ways to increase productivity and raise the standard of living. There has been increasing awareness that improvements depend largely on the willingness of workers – including the growing white-collar groups – to cooperate in a strive for greater efficiency.

The spread of interest in industrial democracy has been matched by a growing awareness of some other closely related administrative issues. The results of technological and economic progress have placed completely new demands on company management and administration, whilst also offering new opportunities and aids. The function of business management has changed essentially during the last few decades and one doesn't have to look far to find the explanation. Look only at the huge size of business enterprises, at the wider markets available, at the effects of mechanization and automation on production techniques and at the increasing dependence on product and market development. Efficient administration and skillful management are regarded increasingly as prerequisites for the welfare of the individual enterprise and of the country as a whole.

A factor not to be forgotten is that the concepts of industrial organization are used nowadays over a broad field. The administrative methods developed in industry and other types of business enterprise, now appear in modified forms in public administration, schools, hospitals, research institutions and other bodies.

Finally comes the fact that all these trends are accompanied by a significant development in the basic theory of business enterprises. From roots in psychology, social psychology, sociology and even in engineering and the natural sciences, an essentially new type of economic and organization theory has been developed.

The purpose of this book is to show that industrial democracy and business organization are not just two subjects which happen to be in the forefront of general discussion; they are closely related. We believe that the problems of industrial democracy can only be adequately understood in the context of modern organization theory.

It is often asserted that a serious obstacle to the discussion of industrial democracy is that different people assign such different meanings to the concept. Indeed, various shades of meaning may be invoked by the same participant at different stages of a debate. In one sense this criticism is certainly justified. Under the heading of industrial democracy a very broad spectrum of questions has been discussed, a great variety of practical solutions have been suggested and widely differing expectations have been expressed.

An official Scandinavian report from 1923 observed that: "... the sometimes rather confused character which discussion of industrial democracy assumes, can be partly explained by the fact that people in various quarters attach such different conceptions to the common name. This same fact also partly explains why the demand for industrial democracy arises from such extremely different sources and why sympathy for the concept can be discovered in widely disparate social groups – groups which seem otherwise diametrically opposed in their views about the ways in which economic life should best develop. When workers belonging to circles often regarded as the most "radical" or "extreme" declare that their future goal is the realization of industrial democracy and when the great American industrial magnate is said to have introduced complete industrial democracy into his companies, it is probably a question of quite different phenomena, albeit stamped with the same name." (The Problems of Industrial Democracy /Den industriella demokratiens problem/, 1923, pp. 18–19. Our translation.)

The complexity of the situation should not, however, be allowed to veil the fact that the debate has a common denominator. It is true that different terms have been used. We have heard about management and employees "working together in a common enterprise" or about "giving the employees a say in the control of their industrial life". But, by and large, the core of the idea has always been the same: to increase employee influence in the management of the company. And although it may not always be explicitly stated, the reference is generally to the rank-and-file employees. The complexity and confusion that we have observed cannot be traced to any real lack of clarity on this point. On the contrary, problems have mainly arisen when it has come to specifying the results desired (or feared) from this influence and to proposing practical courses of action.

To understand the debate about industrial democracy, it is not enough to be able to identify the common denominator – participation in management. It is equally important to realize that, to the various groups concerned, the whole background of aims and means appears in several quite different guises.

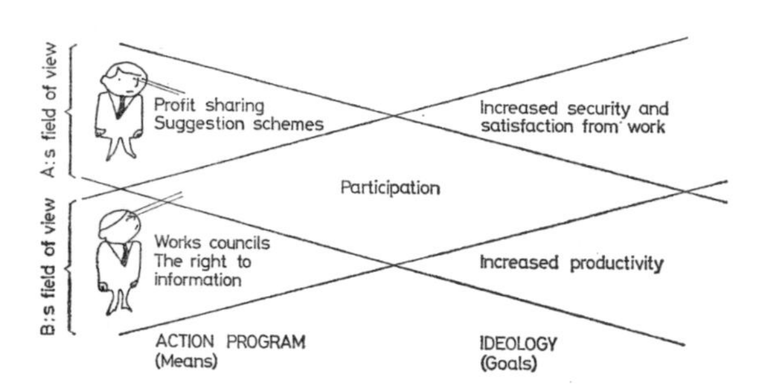

Figure 1. Both A and B regard employee participation in management as desirable. But they are considering quite different courses of action and their ideological goals do not agree.

The situation can be described as in Fig. 1. A method of diagrammatic illustration has been used there which will appear frequently in the following chapters. It is quite possible for A and B in Fig. 1 to agree on what they mean by industrial democracy: that employees should be granted the right to participate in management. They may even agree that participation is desirable. Nonetheless they are quite possibly considering very different practical steps and aiming at quite different goals.

B. THEORY OF ORGANIZATION

The Goals of Industrial Democracy

Most of the themes that have been part of the ideology of industrial democracy in one form or another can be discerned already in the forty-year-old report mentioned earlier. Over the years, however, certain shifts in emphasis have occurred. Sometimes one aspect of the question and sometimes another has been of greater topical interest and received the more attention.

Certainly most people would still grant the importance of what was there called the employees' right to help mould their own working environment and, too, of their right to greater independence and freedom. This is sometimes formulated as a demand for influence on company policy in general and on personnel policy in particular. For many it is probably still natural to make comparisons with developments in other sections of social life and to remark on the disparity between a man's independence inside and outside his place of work.

More too is heard nowadays about employee demands for job satisfaction and general adjustment. While this may in part reflect a shift in terminology, it probably reflects even more the growth of new social values. Much research into the problems of working life now concentrates on just such questions and this in turn has attracted public attention.

Many arguments revolve round the dream of higher productivity and greater efficiency. We can discern here two trains of thought. First it is expected that democratic measures will arouse the employee's interest and cooperation. Secondly it is hoped that if employees have a greater part in running the business, it will be easier to tap their resources of experience, knowledge and ideas. In the long run this should provide the employees themselves with greater opportunities for personal development and education.

Although relations between employee and employer have changed radically in the last forty years, the element of opposition between various groups and between employer and employee is still a subject of much interest. And lively still is the hope then expressed that industrial democracy will be effective to neutralize conflict[1] in working life.

On the other hand we no longer find at the center of the debate the idea of industrial democracy as a first step towards socialization, or as a means of maintaining the existing economic system, or of paving the way to peaceful social and economic development.

[1] For the time being the term conflict is used in the sense of hostile or antagonistic behavior. More precise and slightly different definitions will be given in Chapter 3.

Achieving Industrial Democracy

If we now turn our attention to the various practical programs for realizing the goals of industrial democracy, we find a much greater change between the past and the present. During the first decades of this century keen supporters could still be found for radical solutions, such as syndicalism and various forms of socialism. One of the best known of these was guild socialism as practised in England. It became quite widespread, particularly in the building industry.

In the builders' guilds, of which the first was born around 1920, management was appointed by a trade union or by the workers concerned. Capital was either borrowed or supplied by the customer. In the latter case the builder in charge of the work had considerable control over operations. The price was decided on a basis of the actual time expended, although at a later stage another system was introduced using entrepreneurs and maximum costs.

More recently there have been practically no examples of this type of radical solution, with the emphasis on a more or less complete transfer of the managerial function to the employees. One exception is the Yugoslavian system of workers' councils. However, this really represents an attempt to decentralize a socialized industry. Another possible exception is the central Israeli trade union organization with its extensive involvement in the industry of its country. But this has come about in a very special situation.

Action in most countries has instead been directed towards measures of a more limited kind. Among the most noted are: different types of advisory committees, such as the British works councils; employee representation on the board or in management; extension of share ownership to the employees; profit-sharing.

This survey makes no claim to be complete. But we hope the reader will conclude that both the practical programs and the ideology on which they are based are in fact reasonably well defined. Why is it, then, that so many people, in so many respects, have found the debate confusing?

The Missing Link

One feature typical of many contributions to the debate has been the exclusive interest in means. It has been asked, for instance, whether workers' councils should be advisory or whether they should have some formal right of decision; much has been said for and against profit-sharing; the policy of distributing shares amongst employees has been debated; different systems of representation in management have been compared and many other possible programs have been eagerly debated. Such measures have frequently been discussed but without openly taking stock of the goals involved, goals without which evaluation of the means is impossible and worthless.

It is not surprising to find this particular focus of interest in a debate geared to practical requirements, since it is essentially these which are affected when decisions are made, action taken or countermeasures prepared. At the same time it is likely that in a debate solely or chiefly concerned with concrete measures, arguments can be tough, misunderstandings can easily arise and emotions flare – particularly if the debaters have no common view of the underlying objectives! *Even more confusing has been the lack of scientific theory to throw light on the relations between ends and means.* Instead simple stereotypes and wishful thinking have dominated most attempts at analysis. We can perhaps best illustrate the situation by comparing it with the debate on general economic policy. That this has assumed a more factual character in recent years probably depends, at least in part, on our present possession of a common scientific theory illuminating the relations between the means of economic policy (interest, credit regulation, credit rationing, labor market policy) and its goals (full employment, increased productivity, price stability etc).

The Need for a Common Frame of Reference

We have seen how factual discussions about the problems of industrial democracy, lacking a sound scientific base, have met with severe difficulties. A result of this lack, perhaps equally serious, is that a number of questions may never have been raised at all. Let us look at a few examples. Very little attention has been paid to the question of whether the programs of industrial democracy that have been suggested really form a consistent whole. Are the different subgoals compatible? Are they consistent with the superior goals or with other goals simultaneously accepted? As to the various practical programs, has anybody really probed the question of their success in achieving the goals concerned? And do

they give rise to side effects? If so, what are they? Are there any other more effective ways of reaching the goals?
Rational discussion of a complex problem is often hindered by misunderstandings which easily crop up between the sides taking part. Someone says: "Now we must define our concepts". But very often the purely semantic difficulties are simply the reflection of an even more basic problem; namely that the debaters have essentially different conceptions of what they are discussing. In any analysis of fairly complex phenomena we always have to use radical simplifications – models of the real situation. The model contains concepts corresponding to actual phenomena, together with assumptions about the existence of the phenomena and about the relations between them. Thus two engineers or physicists discussing a technical or scientific problem have the very great advantage that, by reason of their education and training, they have very much the same way of looking at things. They use the same concepts and assign to them more or less the same content; they start from the same basic assumptions; they direct their attention to much the same phenomena and are interested in roughly the same relations.
Without access to some such common viewpoint, it is extremely difficult and perhaps impossible for two people to make contact with each other in a discussion. The debate on industrial democracy provides many examples of this kind of problem. It is easy to list at least a dozen terms commonly in use which can be both vague and ambiguous: responsibility, authority, power, influence, policy, organization, line, staff, freedom, job satisfaction, right of decision, conflict, adjustment etc. There is hardly one basic assumption that can be made without its being questioned; for instance: management is entirely responsible to the owners; the goal of the company is to maximize profit; the individual acts rationally; each employee takes orders from one boss only.

Classical Administration Theory

The drawbacks that we have been discussing appear to have flowed in part from classical administration theory with its emphasis on the formal division of work, accountability, authority and the chain of command. These aspects of organization have been examined with the needs of management in mind. It is quite clear that some of the concepts – and the conclusions – are also used in the debate on industrial democracy, whether or not they are always relevant. We find, for instance, great importance attached to formal authority and the right of decision. "Employee influence on company goals and policy" is another phrase – and a concept – obviously borrowed from the same source. "Let the workers' council play the role of staff adviser to management", claims a supporter of industrial democracy, influenced – perhaps without knowing it – by classical administration theory.

Most of those who nowadays discuss employee participation in management, job satisfaction, adjustment and productivity have similarly drawn their ideas from the "modern" school of administration theory, sometimes called the "human relations movement". The human relations writers were among the first to emphasize that high productivity depends ultimately on job satisfaction and general employee adjustment. They also recognized the importance of keeping employees well informed about what was going on, particularly if changes were being planned. Echoes of these themes are familiar to us from present-day discussion of industrial democracy.

Modern Organization Theory

In recent years the traditional attitude has been criticized on several counts. It has been said that as a theory it is over-simplified and unrealistic, unscientific, empirically unsound and of little practical value. Even if the critics tend in part to exaggerate, it cannot be denied that the image of companies presented by the traditional theory is often so distorted as to be for many purposes downright misleading. The traditional viewpoint is most suitable when:

1. the organizational units are relatively independent of each other,
2. each level in the hierarchy represents successively greater technical and administrative competence,
3. there are comparatively few specialists in the organization,
4. an authoritarian type of management prevails and is accepted by organization members, and
5. the organization functions in a community where stable values and
6. norms pertain and technological development is slow.

These are postulates which conform pretty well with the establishment in most conventional military, religious and industrial organizations. On the other hand the traditional view does not fit well when

1. the organizational units are highly dependent on each other on account of production flow or the use of common resources or for any other technical reason,
2. the functioning of the organization depends on a considerable flow of information between units and in particular when important problem-solving necessarily requires cooperation between several organizational units,
3. as a result of technical and scientific development the boss is often – perhaps almost always – less well informed and less competent to solve the necessary problems and make the necessary decisions, i.e. the concept of the boss as omniscient has become no more than a myth,
4. there are a great many specialists in the organization,
5. as a result of political and economic democracy, authoritarian leadership on the old pattern is no longer accepted by the organization members, and
6. the organization functions in a dynamic community.

In brief, the viewpoint of traditional administration theory seems far from suitable for most large or fairly large modern companies.

However, the past fifteen years has not produced only destructive criticism of old concepts. There have also been constructive attempts to develop a new and more realistic organization theory. It has been pointed out that behavior is controlled or influenced by many different impulses from many different directions. Companies and other organizations are now perceived as systems of components which influence each other in quite a complicated manner. To study the way in which this influence is exerted, it is usual to regard at least some of the organization members or components as the decision makers. This approach brings goals – those of the company and of the individual – and communication problems right into the center of the picture.

A theory of this type does not provide simple rules of behavior of the kind presented in classical administration theory. Instead an attempt is made to describe, explain and predict relations between phenomena. Attention is drawn to the fact that organizations do not always function in the way desired or that things which seem desirable from one angle may not be so from another. Among the phenomena analyzed are conflicts in organizations.

One weakness which the new theory unfortunately shares with the old is that it devotes all too little attention to the differences between one company or organization and another. It seems to be generally accepted, however, that the major part of organization theory applies only to companies which have achieved a certain size, although it has not been possible to say exactly where the boundary lies. Other factors, for example the age of the the company, may also be significant.

For companies with less than ten employees, theories concerning small groups will probably be of greater value than organization theory. When a company has several hundred employees and is fairly long established it has probably reached the stage where organization theory can be applied to it. Between these limits there are bound to be many marginal cases where organization theory will be only partially applicable. However, the fact that the theory presented here is best fitted for relatively large companies need not be such a serious limitation since the debate on industrial democracy seems also to have concentrated on the problems of large enterprises.

THE AIM AND DISPOSITION OF THIS BOOK

This book has developed from the considerations presented above. Consequently we do not start with a clearly defined definition of industrial democracy, but accept the concept as it stands and use it in much the same way that others have done, i.e. as a somewhat ambiguous collective designation for a number of ideological ambitions and political and economic programs.

Throughout most of the book the concrete questions which usually form the substance of the debate on industrial democracy will be mentioned only indirectly. It has already been said that the most serious difficulty in the debate seems to be that we lack the definite starting-point of a scientific theory of organizations. The main purpose of this book will be to try to put together from various sources such a theory.

Following the introductory chapter there will be a section entitled "Theory of Organization" comprising five chapters. Of these, chapter 2

PRINCIPLES OF ORGANIZATION

Objectives

1. The objectives of the enterprise and its component elements should be clearly defined and stated in writing. The organization should be kept simple and flexible.

Activities and grouping of activities

2. The responsibilities assigned to a position should be confined as far as possible to the performance of a single leading function.
3. Functions should be assigned to organizational units on the basis of homogeneity of objective to achieve most efficient and economic operation.

Authority

4. There should be clear lines of authority running from the top to the bottom of the organization, and accountability from bottom to top.
5. The responsibility and authority of each position should be clearly defined in writing.
6. Accountability should always be coupled with corresponding authority.
7. Authority to take or initiate action should be delegated as close to the scene of action as possible.
8. The number of levels of authority should be kept to a minimum.

Relationships

9. There is a limit to the number of positions that can be effectively supervised by a single individual.
10. Everyone in the organization should report to only one supervisor.
11. The accountability of higher authority for the acts of its subordinates is absolute.

Figure 2. An example of the so-called organizational principles. Traditional organization theory has seen as its goal the formulation of such general "commandments". (See Stieglitz, 1961.)

will deal with questions of organization goals and the factors that influence them, chapter 3 will provide a brief study of conflicts in companies and between the stakeholders of a company, chapter 4 will be devoted to the right of decision and other sources of influence, while the complicated tangle of ideas about the relations between leadership style, technology, job satisfaction and productivity will be discussed in chapters 5 and 6.

In the second part of the book, "A Contribution to the Debate", some attempt is made to apply the theory developed here to the discussion of industrial democracy. Some ways in which the various problems could be approached, using this theory, are suggested in chapter 7. In chapter 8 the reader will find some evaluation of the advantages and weaknesses of the theory.

While we know that we cannot provide final answers – in fact, we ask more questions than we answer – we hope that the very fact of analyzing and reformulating some of the old, thorny problems will prove valuable. And perhaps the theory will provide a basis for more systematic discussion and point the way to new lines of enquiry.

CHAPTER 2
THE BALANCE OF INTERESTS IN THE COMPANY
A PRELIMINARY MODEL

INTRODUCTION

Background

The influence of employees on the goals and policy of their company has been one of the most ardently discussed problems of industrial democracy. One side claims, indeed, that the granting of such influence is one of the most important tasks to be tackled. It is often declared that at present influence rests solely with management, owners or anyway the "few" – these are often treated as synonymous – and that justice demands otherwise: capital ownership alone should not determine who "controls companies and makes the decisions but those who offer their labor have also the right to participate" (The Trade Union Movement and Industrial Democracy /Fackföreningsrörelsen och företagsdemokratin/, p. 109. Our translation.)

From the other side comes the objection – apparently based on the same conception of the present situation – that it is unthinkable to give up such fundamental management rights as the freedom to formulate goals and policy; that without concentration of power in the hands of management, the company cannot be efficiently run. To justify this view the special role of risk-bearing capital in the development of the economy is often cited: he who takes the risks should have the right to make the important decisions about managing the business.

One of the reasons for this particular problem receiving so much attention, is certainly that some of the most interesting concrete proposals for realizing industrial democracy have been concerned with it. For instance, at one time there was much interest in the different types of employee representation in management or on the board. In Germany

and partly in Norway, too, such representation has been implemented by legislation. In Sweden interest has come to be focussed mainly on industrial councils and on ways of increasing their powers. The most recent suggestion has been that the councils should become staff organs to advise management on various political and other questions.
One of the most comprehensive developments in the realization of this democratic ideal has been evolved over a period of about twenty years in the well-known Glacier Metal company in close cooperation with the Tavistock Institute in London. At its various centers of operation Glacier Metal has established a legislative system of councils consisting of representatives from management and the various employee groups. They formulate company policy, at the same time guaranteeing that the employees will cooperate loyally in carrying the policy through.

The Aim and Contents of the Chapter

In the past discussion has undoubtedly concentrated on the conflict between employee demands for influence and management claims to freedom in policy-making. It is therefore extremely interesting to note in modern organization theories the emphasis on evaluating company goals and policy. What are goals and policy? How do they – or how should they – come about? Who does – or who should – influence them? The various ideas now coming to maturity are the fruits of an interplay between economic theory and sociological research and suggest a change from many earlier beliefs.
In this chapter we intend to provide a brief survey of the theory about company goals and policy. We start with a general description of the situation in large modern Scandinavian companies and explain some of the terms used. One of our purposes is to show how very complex the circumstances actually are, and in this way justify the following formal analysis. To begin this, we define some concepts and discuss briefly the function of goals and policy in a company. We then suggest a theory about their formulation.

COMPANY GOALS AND POLICY – SOME EXAMPLES

The terms "goals" and "policy" are in frequent use in companies and in

economic literature but no very deep analysis is needed to show that both terms are vague and are often employed in widely differing senses.
It is usually assumed in classical economic theory that a company's goal is to maximize profit. Many have questioned this, others have suggested alternatives or modifications on the lines of "in the long run". However, this fundamental postulate was largely the child of the mathematic tools available at its birth. As differential and integral calculus have lost ground to the more fashionable linear programming and game theory, when "profit maximizing" is allowed as a goal, it is hedged around with restrictions and references to "gaming behavior".
An oft repeated principle of good organization is that "the company's operations should have a clearly defined goal known to all members of the organization" (cf. fig. 2, p. 1/12). What is meant by this is not quite clear and a study of the principle as applied in practice reveals many interpretations. One is to try to summarize the "basic" goals of the company in a few short phrases and an investigation made a few years ago revealed that this has become common in large American companies. Our own experience confirms that the situation in many Scandinavian firms is similar. The following is a typical example:

"Brunswick's objective is to improve constantly its service in all fields, ever searching for a means of expanding these services, developing new ones to benefit our customers, analyzing their requirements and heeding their needs – constantly to improve quality.
To plan long-range growth of Brunswick and to operate at a profit.
To recognize dignity of the individual and to provide Brunswick people with the necessary opportunity and incentive for maximum self-expression and growth.
To provide steady employment at wages equal to or better than community rates for comparable service.
Maintain pleasant work surroundings and to provide the best equipment and methods to accomplish a given task." (Thompson, 1958)

Other companies have tried to fulfill this "principle of good organization" by working out concrete long-range programs. These usually cover five-year, ten-year or perhaps twenty-year periods and provide the basis for short-range planning and budgeting.
The principle is often taken a step further by trying to formulate goals for organizational units as well as for the company as a whole. This means that goals have been set for product areas, markets etc or for functions.
But "goals" is an ambiguous term: it might refer either to a very general

goal, to a concrete current program, to an overall goal or to a goal for one part of the organization. But the term lends itself to variety in other respects too. A goal can be a written goal without any influence on actual behavior, the goal as applied in practice, the goal that is actually achieved, the employees' conception of a goal, the concrete ambitions of the president or the top management group, the hopes of the owners or society's view of what ought to be the goal of the company.
Furthermore the terms "goal" and "policy" are sometimes used as almost synonymous. For example, one company states that their *goal* is to "be able to give the employees good wages and social benefits; good, secure working conditions and the greatest possible security of tenure", whilst another formulates the same ambition in terms of policy: "The *policy* of this company is to provide the employees with good wages...".
In general, however, the term policy or *company* policy is used for the more detailed rules which prescribe the means that are considered legitimate or essential in the fulfillment of a superior goal (e.g. survival). During recent decades many companies have devoted much attention to the question of the value of a codified policy. Many companies have produced quite comprehensive manuals which in fact often consist of a set of rules for behavior in particular situations plus definitions of important economic and organizational terms. Sales policy has provided basic rules for behavior towards customers; purchasing policy has regulated behavior in relation to suppliers; personnel policy has provided a complement to the collective agreements and to the conditions of service by regulating in rather more general terms company behavior towards employees.
Various arguments have been put forward in support of codified company policies. It has been claimed that there is a whole range of important questions in the running of a company which cannot be decided on the basis of a purely factual analysis. These are in the nature of ethical questions and it is the duty of management to examine and define its attitude towards them. Further management is compelled from time to time to take a stand on different questions which nevertheless have so much in common that they could be decided upon in principle once and for all, thus becoming an ingredient of the company's codified policy. Many other perhaps rather unexpected arguments have been put forward; for instance that it is extremely educative for all those concerned to try

to examine important questions of principle so fundamentally that a written answer can be produced.

In most companies, however, and particularly in small ones, the term "policy" refers to something considerably more informal. It may be applied to a statement once made by a superior which has subsequently come to be regarded as a guiding line for others of lower rank. It may be an informal norm – a term we shall discuss in detail later – which has developed in a particular group. It might reflect a conscious effort on the part of a subordinate to try to interpret, from the various statements and information reaching him from time to time, "what the company's policy really is".

SOME CONCEPTS AND THEIR DEFINITIONS

The Goal of the Company

It has sometimes been claimed by sociologists that there is no such thing as the goal of a company or of an organization; that, basically, the only type of goal is that of the individual; the concept of the group goal is a leftover from earlier assumptions about the existence of a "group spirit". A few empirical studies have been made, however, and these confirm what the above examples have already shown: that in companies and other organizations there is generally considerable agreement concerning certain common goals and that much attention has been paid to the task of formulating and working them out in detail. The fact that such extreme differences of opinion can exist, reflects the prevailing confusion in the use of the terms "goals" and "policy". In order to provide a basis for a systematic discussion of the subject, we can begin by defining some concepts in more detail.

The sociological concept of *function* constitutes a convenient starting-point for a theory. By the *function of an organization* is meant the objective consequences of the organization's existence and activities in relation to a particular, carefully defined broader system. For instance the function of the LKAB Mining Company in relation to Sweden is to provide employment in the far north of the country, to improve the balance of trade and to provide the government (who owns the company) with revenue. The company's main function in relation to the yet broader system of Western Europe is to provide a reliable supply of cheap, high quality iron ore.

In contrast to the concept of the organization's function, which concerns the objective consequences of its behavior, the concept of the organization's *goal* has to be related to what the individual organization member or outside observer would like the consequences of its activities to be. It is possible for the goal, thus conceived, and the function to be similar or even identical; they may on the other hand be quite different or even conflicting. From the point of view of society, the company's function is to produce goods, to provide employment and occasionally to handle and take care of housing, education and so on. At the same time the company's goal may be regarded by its management primarily as survival by exploiting existing markets, expanding into new markets or by other means.

The term *goal* according to this definition is always concerned with the conceptions of an individual or a group. It is thus important to indicate whose goal conceptions are relevant in any particular context: those of top management, department managers, workers, trade union leaders, visiting scientists – we could continue this list ad infinitum.

In view of this it must be wrong, at any rate as regards nomenclature, to use the term "goal" without qualification or classification. The fact that the expression "the company's goal" is employed in the literature becomes explicable only if we regard it as an abbreviation of, for example, "management's conception of the company's goal" or "the owner's conception of the company's goal". In general this is perhaps an acceptable explanation. The following view is, however, more precise.

In economics the company is regarded as a unit. It is assumed that company behavior can be explained in much the same way as an individual's behavior; the organization is conceived as a single decision-maker and its goal as that of a single representative. Significantly this assigns the "goal of the organization" to the role of a theoretical concept without any direct counterpart in reality. At least in large companies, whose behavior is the result of decisions made by many individuals, there will only very exceptionally be much similarity between "the goal of the organization" and the goal of the individual. Research has shown with increasing conviction that to explain behavior in large companies it is necessary to study the factors influencing individual decision-making. Top managers are certainly very important, but those of lower status and the rank and file employees cannot be ignored.

In a later chapter dealing with the theory of leadership we will elaborate the factors controlling the behavior of the individual organization member. For the time being let it suffice to say that somehow, in one form or another, management will establish and prescribe goals for the company, with a view to coordinating its own decision-making and influencing that of its subordinates.

To sum up, instead of the simple concept of the organization's goal, we must distinguish at least three essentially different concepts, i.e.

1. the purely theoretical construct "the goal of the organization",
2. the individual member's conception of the goal of the organization, and
3. the goals prescribed by management.

And as regards policy, similar distinctions must be recognized. In order to avoid this ambiguity in the meaning of the term "policy", we will now introduce the term norm.

Norms

We shall use the concept of "*norm*" as a collective term for all types of behavioral rules and rules for evaluation of behavior. In the company, norms are given such names as policies, directives, routines, instructions, procedures and the like.

As in the case of goals, it is possible to distinguish between norms as a conception of organization members and norms as prescribed or codified. In the latter form they can be prescribed by an individual or group, usually in a position of superiority; these may be intended for another group, usually in a subordinate position, or again they may be intended for the group that has prescribed them. Norms may be the result of other norms prevailing in a wider sphere, for example, a whole concern, a whole industry, a whole nation or a whole culture.

Norms can range from prescribed legal codes to informal rules. Their character may be that of a scale of preference, prescribing what is good, better and best or bad, worse and worst. They may indicate desirable behavior in detailed terms or they may forbid behavior of a particuar kind.

Plans

Also very important in a company and related to both goals and norms, are plans. A prescribed plan is, like a norm, a blue-print of desired future behavior. A plan differs from a norm in that it is not generalized; it is concerned with a single and usually fixed occasion or a limited number of occasions. Apart from this, plans can in general be classified in much the same way as norms. In practice it is often difficult to determine whether a particular rule is to be regarded and treated as a plan or as a norm.

Goals, Norms and Plans in a Complex Network

We shall see later how goals, norms and plans arise. Meanwhile it is important to remember that they are often dependent on each other, usually forming a hierarchy in which certain of them derive from certain others. Similarly, organization members do not only think in terms of the company as a whole or in long-range perspective. They are also aware of special norms, subgoals, short-term plans etc. which apply to their own department or group. Thus, what one member regards as a plan may to another be a goal, and a goal for short-term operations may also be one item in a long-range plan.
From this we can see that the overall picture in an organization of any size will generally be extremely intricate. Scientists no longer consider it particularly fruitful or realistic to suppose that a system can actually exist in which all subgoals can be derived from one single, fundamental goal. Furthermore it is now recognized that goals, norms and plans – and in particular the relative importance that is assigned to different aspects of them – vary with time. What is felt at one time to be of major importance may have sunk back into relative insignificance after only a few weeks or even a few days.
For the individual organization member the situation is simpler. He probably knows only a few of the goals, plans and norms in any detail. Of some others he may have a general, often extremely simplified, picture and of yet others he may be totally ignorant.

Why Prescribe Goals, Norms and Plans?

Management tries more or less consciously and systematically, to see that organization members have the same conceptions of goals, norms and plans. If they have, coordination will function well and efficiency be well served.

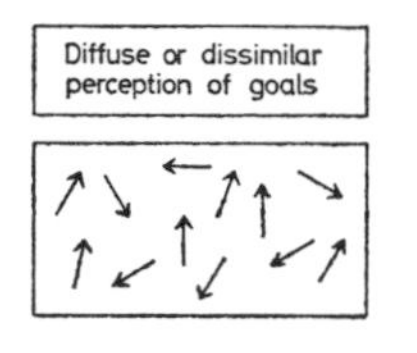

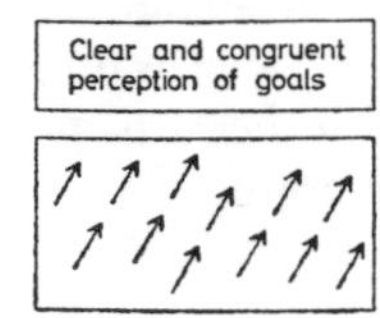

Figure 3. The effect of similar conceptions of goals, norms and plans has been compared with the effect of a magnetic field. All the organization members can be attracted into a cohesive pattern.

The way in which organizations accomplish their various goals is often remarkably impressive, for example that it should ever be possible to coordinate the efforts of several thousands of people to produce, for instance, an aeroplane or an atomic reactor. A rather more detailed study of the organization at work will reveal further grounds for respect; it is not only the manufacturing process which requires cooperation from a great many organization members; throughout the organization the administration also calls for the coordination of numerous decisions on questions large and small. That this coordination is possible depends chiefly on the members accepting the prescribed goals, norms and plans as a basis for their decision-making.

It is not a simple matter to impose on all employees the same conceptions of the goals, norms and plans of an organization. Nor does management always seek to force its prescriptions on the other employees; very often the situation is the opposite, with subordinates eagerly seeking guidance from above. They may ask outright what the goals and policy of the company "really" are; or maybe they simply try to interpret the behavior and decisions of the boss. The reason is simple. There are many situations in which the individual decision-maker, whether he be departmental manager or rank and file employee, cannot find sufficient guidance from his own goals and ambitions or from the norms that he holds as a member of a community or a culture. If he is to make adequate decisions he will have to ask himself "what are the company's goals and norms?"

For this reason among others the organization member who does feel that he has a clear idea and understanding of the organization's goals, norms and plans will possess a considerable source of security and satisfaction. Such an understanding is likely to raise the standard of work and help to counteract conflicts.

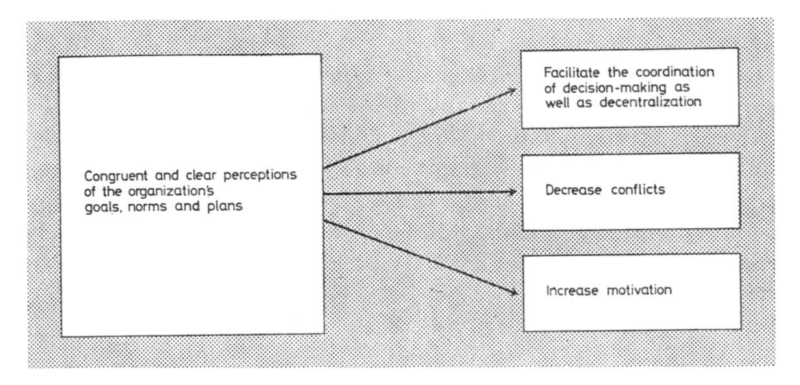

Figure 4. Agreement as to the content of goals, norms and plans has many beneficial effects.

HOW DOES MANAGEMENT REGULATE GOALS, NORMS AND PLANS?

In companies of any size management will try to work out and prescribe goals and rules in such a way that members' conception of norms and programs will agree.

When supporters of industrial democracy claim that employees should participate in formulating goals and policy, it is probably these management-made rules that they have in mind. If we are to understand exactly what the demand involves, it is not enough to explain what is meant by goals and policy. We must also try to find out how they arise.

Before embarking on a closer analysis of this question, it should be emphasized yet once more that not all the conceptions of goals, norms and plans which exist in an organization have their origin or even their counterpart in the rules prescribed by management. Even in companies where management devotes much attention to the systematic analysis and formulation of goals, norms and plans, it is generally only practicable to compose a limited number of basic rules. And even then the term "management" must be understood in a very broad sense. It is by no means only top management which is involved in working out the rules. Committees and working groups consisting of representatives from different organs in the company may also be used. Sometimes works councils or similar units contribute, in which case the employee or trade union representatives will act as adviser. In other cases an outsider is employed as consultant. And, lastly, great scope in formulating details is often left to managers and supervisors at a lower level.

An organization also has to make room for a vast complex of norms from quite other sources. An important group consists of norms based on general social standards, either as defined by law or accepted by custom. These often apply equally to management, office staff and workers, but they can sometimes have greater relevance for a particular group. General norms concerning honesty, politeness, justice and loyalty to the company are examples of the first type, while certain norms for the behavior of a boss or a subordinate represent the second.

Even where rules have been formulated by management, it is far from certain that they will be followed in the company. If the regulations are to influence behavior they must at least be known to the employees and be regarded as authoritative and acceptable. From management's point of view the ideal is that employees so identify themselves with the company and its management that they accept the prescribed goals, norms and plans as their own. But to suppose that this usually is the case would be as wrong as to assume that it is never so, and despite all the limitations discussed here, it would not be realistic to underrate the significance of management-made rules. We may now examine what factors affect their formulation.

The Company and its Stakeholders

Relatively few companies are newly established. Most have behind them a history, some quite a long one. This provides an excellent opportunity for exploring the ways in which an established management formulates new goals and rules in a changing situation. Certain operations are already under way; the employees have certain conceptions of their goals and about the norms and plans that are relevant. How are new developments dovetailed into existing ones?

We shall be using the term *stakeholders* to designate the individuals or groups which depend on the company for the realization of their personal goals and on whom the company is dependent. In that sense employees, owners, customers, suppliers, creditors as well as many other groups can all be regarded as stakeholders in the company. Management can also be counted among them – initially we shall ignore the case, admittedly common, where owner and manager are identical. Even the community as a whole, both state and local, can be regarded as a stakeholder since the company is dependent on society and society on the company.

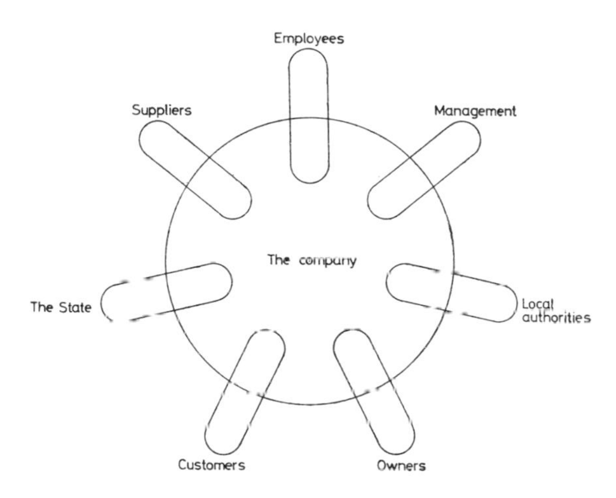

Figure 5. The stakeholders in an organization are the individuals or groups dependent on the company for the realization of their personal goals and on whom the company is dependent for its existence.

To summarize: it is a characteristic of stakeholders that they place demands on the company and the company has claims on them. Later we shall analyze the several factors governing these claims, of which an important one is the goals and needs of the stakeholders. Some claims are economic: the employees expect wages, the suppliers payment, the creditors and owners interest and dividends. In the case of the employees, however, it is well established that the financial advantage is by no means the only factor deciding whether or not they will stay with the company. The same is probably true in varying degrees of other categories of stakeholder. Each one of them forms certain expectations, based on their conceptions of the company's goals and plans, of the likelihood of their claims being fulfilled. Depending upon the urgency of their claims and their knowledge of alternative ways of fulfilling them, the stakeholders will decide whether or not their expectations are likely to be achieved.

In most cases, the stakeholders are voluntary members of the organization. The employees can leave the company and take other positions.

The capitalists may contrive to transfer their investments to other companies. The customers and suppliers can transfer their business elsewhere and the community can remove its support and give it to another company, another type of company, another form of enterprise etc. Stakeholders are more likely to sever their association if the company's expected future behavior seems unlikely to allow for the satisfaction of the stakeholders' own claims.

We mentioned above that management can be regarded as a stakeholder. For many reasons, however, it is in a unique position since it has also to act as a mediator, resolving conflicts between the stakeholders and sometimes even deciding which claims will be satisfied. Moreover, management is usually the group most inclined to identify itself with the organization and to fight for its survival, expansion and future security. There are many possible reasons for this: of all the stakeholders, management has perhaps most difficulty in transferring its commitment from one company to another, particularly if the first company has not been very successful; furthermore there seems to be a close correlation between the size of the company and the remuneration of the management.

Management – Everybody's Puppet?

As can be understood from our earlier description of management's position, there is often very little freedom of action when it comes to formulating goals, norms and plans. Quite apart from the limitations imposed by various technical factors – plans and rules of behavior must after all be practicable – management will find that it cannot realize its own goals without taking into consideration the claims of the many other stakeholders. The manager's chief role will be to interpret the needs of the situation, striking a balance between the often conflicting demands of the various interests, so that the organization can survive. In the skilful handling of these factors he also sees the best chance of fulfilling his own ambitions.

In one of the most comprehensive empirical studies ever made of the work of the business leader, one writer summarized his impressions in the following colourful words:

> "Before we made the study, I always thought of a chief executive as the conductor of an orchestra, standing aloof on his platform. Now I am in some respects inclined to see him as the puppet in a puppet-show with hundreds of people pulling the strings and forcing him to act in one way or another".
> (Carlson, 1951, p. 52).

The notion of the business leader as one whose sole ambition is that his company should survive and, if possible, expand, is of course oversimplified. Among the personal goals of the leader are a varying mixture of crass and idealistic motives: to make money; to get things done; to be a success; to be a good citizen, a good colleague and a popular boss. Filling out the picture in this way serves to emphasize still more how dependent the business leader is on good relations with the other stakeholders.

No picture of the situation would be complete without some mention of the fact that stakeholders who wish to exert influence on the business leader have many sanctions at their disposal other than a refusal to give the company their support. For example employees can strike, politicians can threaten restrictive measures or several groups can ally themselves to assert their claims. Furthermore, all categories – customers, employees and society – have come to rely increasingly on the social pressure of public opinion.

These several questions will be discussed in more detail in chapter 3.

Are there Different Types of Leadership?

It is sometimes claimed that business leaders differ fundamentally in the way they balance the claims of the various stakeholders. We can indicate two extreme types.

First we have the type of leader – and many authors think that this is the predominating kind – who is not too willing to formulate clear, long-range goals. Problems are dealt with as they arise. The daily decisions result in a pattern of behavior which could best be described as a process of trial and error. If a business leader of this type is asked what goals have guided the development of his company, a fairly honest answer would be: "it just happened that way".

At the other extreme we have the type of business leader who, with great precision and purpose, formulates long-range goals for his company. He formulates what has sometimes been called a mission and to realize this mission he is prepared to abstain from many incidental opportunities and to fight many a fierce tussle with the stakeholders whose claims, at any rate in the short run, may not always be fulfilled.

It has been declared by many writers that this last type of leadership is always the most successful, but there is little or no empirical basis for such a claim. Clearly formulated goals can have many advantages, particularly in so far as they promote coordination and stimulate enthusiasm. At the same time it has been shown that they can lead to inflexibility which, in a changing environment, may even jeopardize survival. The description below of management's problem-solving technique is chiefly applicable to the type of leader who inclines more towards adaptation to the claims of the various stakeholders.

Management's Problem-solving Technique

When goals, norms and plans are to be formulated, the least exacting course is to continue in the same way as before, namely with the old goals and the same rules. Empirical research has confirmed that there is a condition in companies which could be called a state of natural inaction. We might say that the much cherished management-by-exception principle represents inaction raised to the status of a law. According to this principle management is supposed to devote all its resources to the "acute" problems. Only when a new situation or an additional claim from the stakeholders arises or an increase in ambition on the part of management renders the earlier rules inadequeate, are they exposed to any revision. Moreover, the revision will probably apply only to limited sections of the whole extensive hierarchy of goals, norms and plans. An overall re-examination will be rare indeed.

Most companies, however, exist in a rapidly changing environment. More or less regularly they are called upon to face new and greater claims from those with an interest in their affairs. The employees want more wages, the customers demand higher quality, society increases its claims and so on. Although inaction may be the natural condition for management, a re-examination of at least parts of the company program will be an unavoidable necessity.

In the re-examination at least three types of process can be distinguished: means-end analysis, innovation and the resolution of conflicts between the various stakeholders.

A *means-end analysis* is a purely factual investigation. The suitability of various rules or alternative courses of action are tested or reassessed in relation to certain superior goals, norms or plans. In other words the relation between different levels in the goal hierarchy is reviewed in the light of fresh developments. Perhaps new or more complete information has become available and it is possible to evaluate more accurately the consequences of alternative courses of action.

Suppose, for example, that a company's prescribed sales goal has been to maintain the share of the market and at the same time to increase profitability. The means to achieve this goal have been formulated, for instance to bring down selling costs by improving efficiency whilst maintaining sales efforts (measured in number of customer visits, total publicity etc). Perhaps for one reason or another sales results have not been so good and the suitability of the short-term goal begins to be questioned. It will then be necessary to consider and compare alternative short-term goals.

The means-end analysis presupposes that there are alternative goals, norms or plans with which to make a comparison. In the case quoted, one alternative might be to raise prices and improve the efficiency of the sales organization. If no immediately available alternatives are acceptable, then one will have to be found. This is what is meant by *innovation*. Innovation can occur at all levels in the goal hierarchy. Sometimes a considerable change in operations may be involved, for example a changeover from agency selling to running a full sales organization, the introduction of new products, the development of new markets or the introduction of new production methods. Generally, however, the changes are on a lesser scale, for example, altering some feature of a

product, introducing a new type of discount for a certain class of customer or reorganizing quality control.
Methods by which management seeks to resolve conflicts between stakeholders will be discussed in the next chapter.

Profit Maximizing and the Efficiency Norm[1]

One of the most common subjects of dispute in any discussion of company goals is whether the only ,or at any rate the main, goal of all private companies is to maximize profits. Classical economic theory assumes this to be true and many people still claim that it is so – even in fact that it *should* be so.
Why does this article of faith die so hard, although it is obviously often without substance? One of the main reasons is that profit is a tangible sign of management's success. It shows that resources have been carefully managed and some at any rate of the stakeholder's claims satisfied. And management can point to further yield which is being ploughed back into the company.
But another reason for the honor still paid to profit maximization is that it provides a ready measure of efficiency. Since the efficiency norm is so deeply rooted in Western culture, this fact is very important. Breaches of the norm are regarded as almost immoral and it is not generally difficult to get most of the employees in a company to accept it at least in principle. High profits can easily be cited as proof that their efforts have not been in vain.
However, to strive for efficiency, eschewing waste and carelessness is by no means necessarily the same as to strive for maximization of profits in the sense implied in economic theory. It cannot of course be denied that companies probably do exist where the owner's power to appoint and dismiss management is so great, or where the business leader so identifies himself with the owners' interests, that profit maximization does become the predominating goal. Whether this is a usual situation

[1] This discussion of profit and efficiency applies particularly to Sweden where for instance the Trade Unions have openly declared that companies or industries which because of inefficiency or other reasons are unable to produce a profit should not be allowed to continue operations. This has been motivated by an understanding of the connection between efficiency and ability to pay high wages.

only further empirical research can show. Results available hitherto are far from conclusive.

EMPLOYEE INFLUENCE ON COMPANY GOALS AND POLICY

Up to this point our discussion has produced the general conclusion that employees are one of the groups that influence company goals and policy but that management and specialists are usually responsible for formulating the prescribed goals. Putting a rather unusual slant on it, we have expressed it thus: management and its assistants have a special position, mainly in that they function as interpreter of the demands of the situation and as creator of a program acceptable to all; at the same time the employees and their organizations are one of the pressure groups which affect what management will regard as the "demands of the situation". From this point of view it is difficult to see any difference between, for example, employees and capitalists.

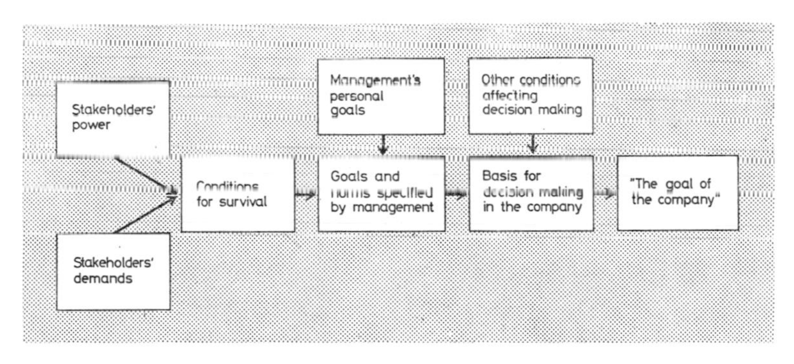

Figure 6. Summary of the theory of the company's goals and policy.

A general discussion about "how to give the employee some influence on company goals and policy" is therefore misleading: it implies that such influence does not at present exist. For many reasons, however, this part of the ideology of industrial democracy is often expressed in that way. There may be a misunderstanding of reality here. Or it may be that the formulation is a tactical one and that its strategy – the real significance behind it – is a demand for *more* influence for the employees.

It may be an expression of dissatisfaction with the *forms* of influence. Or perhaps "restrictive influence" – the right to say "no" – is not considered enough and "creative influence" – the right to participate in working out practical programs – is also required. Finally the search for new forms of employee influence on company goals and policy may really reflect a desire not so much for increased influence but for more understanding of the common goals and greater loyalty from the employees.

CHAPTER 3
THE BALANCE OF INTERESTS IN THE COMPANY COOPERATION AND CONFLICT

INTRODUCTION

Conflict – a Social Ill

From the early days of industrialization and of the labor movement, conflict between employer and employees has been a marked social phenomenon. At the same time many writers in the social sciences as well as many representing various political doctrines have seen such conflict and antagonism in a wider context. They have set before us a picture of a degenerate society on the verge of collapse. In his criticism of eighteenth century capitalism Marx was one of a motley company of writers, all as extreme as himself, who in their different ways regarded conflict as something fundamental and explosive. Even the pioneers of industrial psychology, such as Mayo, were much concerned by the problem of conflict.

". . . the requirement of a sound social organization is the spontaneous cooperation of its members within the various enterprises in which they are organized. Conflict in human society, and especially political conflict, is always a symptom of social disease". (Bendix & Fisher, 1949, p. 114.)

With this starting-point, the industrial psychologists naturally felt deeply committed to removing the cause of conflict as an essential to curing the malady. Many of them even thought they had found solutions. The introduction of democracy into working life has often been regarded as just such a remedy for this serious social ill.

Although the situation in Scandinavia as in many other countries has changed essentially during the last few decades and the problem no longer has the same extreme urgency the attitude towards conflict remains the same. Conflict is still commonly regarded as the sign of some shortcoming in the social system.

The Aim and Contents of the Chapter

In the previous chapter we described the conflict between employer and employees in a way which is hardly compatible with its reputation as a sympton of social ill. To begin with, it was shown that the usual type of conflict on the labor market should not be regarded chiefly as between the company or the management and the employees, but rather as an expression for the conflicting demands made by the workers and the other stakeholders, perhaps in particular the customers and owners. Secondly, it was pointed out that it is hardly realistic to hope for a complete cessation of conflict. Clashes may arise simply because it is not possible to give everybody everything they want; conflict is therefore more or less independent of political or economic systems.

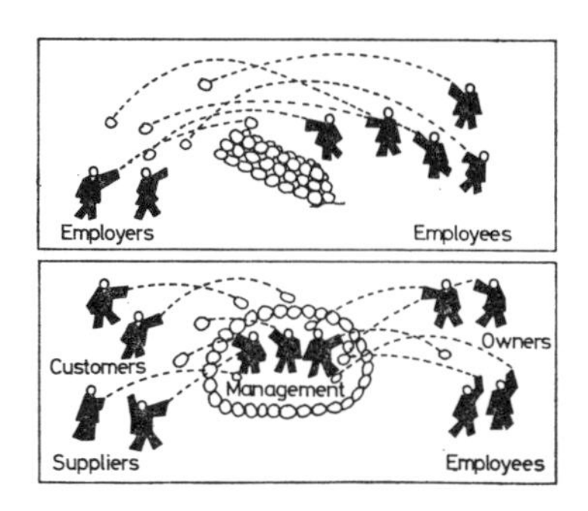

Figure 7. According to the theory developed in the previous chapter, the traditional view of a hostile relationship between employer and employees can be replaced by a conception of management as defender of the company against the claims of the stakeholders.

These themes will be developed in greater detail in this chapter. The concept of conflict will be further analyzed and the argument put forward not only that conflicts are unavoidable; very often they are even to be welcomed. The starting-point for this discussion is the same basic model of the company that we used in the previous chapter. We shall try to examine the progress of a conflict, making a closer study of the mechanisms by which the company stakeholders hope to bring pressure to bear and the means available to them, and of the methods employed by management as arbitrator and middleman. We shall also develop a theory which should enable us to forecast the chances open to the various persons and groups of satisfying their demands during – or as a result of – a conflict. This will provide us with an opportunity to discuss in a little more detail such questions as the type and amount of influence wielded by employees and ways in which this influence can be increased or diminished.

A THEORY – THE POINT OF DEPARTURE

Marx saw social conflict as an inevitable consequence of the capitalist system, a sure sign of approaching collapse. The followers of the human relations movement were as firmly committed in their way, emotionally convinced that conflict was needless. These and other extremist views have been gradually replaced in modern science by a more finely distinctive approach.

It has been assumed, to begin with, that conflict is a normal social phenomenon. Scientists have then asked: why do conflicts arise and what affects their existence, their frequency and their character? Also, importantly, theories have been developed about the course of conflicts. At the same time the simple view has been abandoned that conflicts are undesirable and, instead, attempts have been made to explain their effects in different contexts. Many of these are functional, that is, essential to the functioning of the social system whilst others are disruptive to the functioning of the social system, that is dysfunctional.

It is not possible to present here a complete history of the development of conflict theory. In fact, it is misleading to speak of "the" theory as of something which is consistent and generally accepted. What follows must, even more than elsewhere in this book, be regarded as a subjective selection of – and in some degree as one more attempt to reconcile – the various propositions.

First, however, a few comments on the origin of modern conflict theories. Sociological theorists have done much to broaden the general understanding of conflicts, and Social Psychology has provided valuable experimental and other empirical material. Game theory, an offshoot of economic theory, has made it possible to refine considerably such basic concepts as conflict, party, outcome etc. Recently, chiefly as a result of research into economic theory, an essentially new line of approach has developed. The point has been made that a situation characterized purely by conflict very rarely occurs. Much more usual is some kind of combination of conflict and a need to cooperate: one party's chances of achieving his goals depend partly on the ability to win over his opponent and partly on the ability to cooperate with him.

The theory which we present below concerns a situation of exactly this type, characterized by three conditions as described in chapter 2:

1. the parties involved in the conflict have a common interest in the survival of the company,
2. institutionalized cooperation, i.e. cooperation in accordance with certain fixed rules, has been established to promote the satisfaction of common interests and to solve problems arising from conflicting ones,
3. a special group, management, devotes itself professionally to resolving the conflicts and maintaining the cooperation.

It should be observed that our theory is not a general one. It cannot, for instance, be applied as it stands to conflicts between nations or to conflicts among the employees in a company.

COMMON AND CONFLICTING INTERESTS IN THE COMPANY

In the previous chapter we defined organizations – with particular emphasis on those usually known as business enterprises or companies – as socio-technical systems, depending for their existence on various individuals, groups and other organizations. The latter were jointly designated the company's stakeholders. It was further stated that the stakeholders are dependent on the organization for achieving their goals.

Because of their commitment to the company, the stakeholders become dependent on each other. The behavior of one stakeholder will affect in many ways the opportunities of the others.

The most usual forms of mutual dependence are two. First, the contributions of the stakeholders are interdependent and must be coordinated if they are to be employed effectively. Such coordination is in the common interest of the stakeholders. Secondly, the stakeholders are dependent on each other because the claims that they make on the company are to some extent conflicting. The suppliers demand a long term of delivery, the customers a short one. The employees want convenient working hours, the customers want service. The owners hope for profit, the

customers for low prices and the employees for high wages, etc. Also, one stakeholder may play more than one role – an employee is perhaps also a customer or a supplier – thus further complicating the pattern.
Relations between stakeholders are in fact characterized by the simultaneous existence of conflicting and common interests. The common interests will result in attempts towards cooperation and coordination. The existence of a *conflict of interests* will often complicate and sometimes even obstruct cooperation.
A conflict of interests often becomes significant only when those concerned are conscious of it. It will be assumed without further discussion here that in any given situation the stakeholders in the company are conscious of this element of conflict.
The opposing forces – the need for cooperation versus the assertion of conflicting interests – are continually at work. If the company is to survive, it is necessary that the first of these gain the upper hand, that cooperation be achieved and maintained, despite the unavoidable conflicts of interest. This is made possible by a more or less continuous process, to be analyzed in more detail later, which we will here call *conflict resolution*. The designation does not imply that the conflicts of interest have disappeared but simply that cooperation has been achieved despite them.
But even in a situation where cooperation has once been established, it may fail at a later stage. After all, organizations usually exsist in changing situations, if for no other reason than because the claims of the stakeholders rarely remain constant for long. According to one theory, these claims tend to form levels of aspiration, which are being adjusted almost continuously – in our type of society, generally to a higher level. Normally employees demand wage increase, customers require better quality and suppliers higher prices.
When the conflict resolution is unsuccessful, it is said that an *acute conflict* has arisen. By this is meant that cooperation is temporarily obstructed or has ceased altogether. Perhaps a stakeholder, alone or with others, withdraws his contribution to the organization, partly or entirely, or perhaps applies other sanctions (strikes, decreased quality of deliveries etc). The difference between the continuous process of adjustment and the acute conflict should not be exaggerated. The acute conflict is often more sensational and has emotional overtones. But in fact it is nothing more

than an expression of the fact that for the time being the conflict resolution has not as yet achieved success. We shall see later that it can even be regarded as one phase in the process of conflict resolution.

It is important to emphasize that, in accordance with the usage of conflict theory, the concept of conflict has been given a wider meaning here than it has in common parlance[1]. When the man in the street discusses, for instance, conditions on the labor market and uses terms such as "conflict" and "measures against conflict", he usually means strikes, lockouts etc, or what we have here called acute conflicts. According to our definitions there is always a state of conflict in a company since the stakeholders have conflicting goals.

COOPERATION AND CONFLICT AT DIFFERENT LEVELS

Cooperation and coordination are such fundamental features of organizations that they are often used as defining characteristics. Cooperation appears in many forms and, we feel justified in saying, at different levels.

Cooperation of the various resources is made possible in part by what we have called the stakeholders' commitment to the organization. Economic theory has often dwelt upon cooperation at this level.

At more detailed levels, contributions and activities within the organization are coordinated in different ways, for instance by cultivating among the members some conception of the common goals, plans and norms. This was discussed in the previous chapter.

Again, within the framework of these goals, norms and plans, the behavior of the individual members is further coordinated. For this purpose management has developed a multitude of aids. Important examples are the relaying of orders "down the line", the use of staff specialists, mechanical aids such as the conveyor belt and various types of planning systems.

Although cooperation and coordination may be impeded at all these levels by conflicts of interest, we shall concentrate almost entirely in this chapter on cooperation and conflict at the first level, that which directly concerns the stakeholders' involvement in the company. Coordination

[1] As will be explained later, the term *negotiation* too will be used in a sense other than that usually employed in everyday language.

and conflict within the organization and between individual organization members is reserved until chapters 5 and 6.

INSTITUTIONALIZED CONFLICT RESOLUTION

If we study the methods used for resolving conflicts and establishing cooperation between the stakeholders of a company, we find not only a widely assorted collection but also quite definite rules about the methods which can and should be used in different types of situation. One aspect of these rules is that they reveal very definite expectations on the part of the stakeholders about how the opposing party is to behave in the interaction that is supposed to lead to a resolution. It is therefore possible, using an accepted sociological terminology to refer to these rules and mutual expectations as institutions for conflict resolution.

The first rudimentary theory on this subject is little more than an attempt to produce a scheme of classification. It has thus been suggested that certain main types of institutions or methods are available to the stakeholders for the establishment of cooperation. Here we shall consider three of them: the market, joint decisionmaking and cooptation. In all these management plays the part of arbitrator or middleman and functions as the representative of the stakeholders in general vis à vis a particular one of them, for example the employees.

We shall now describe these institutions, having first reminded the reader that they are theoretical examples of phenomena which in reality rarely appear in the clearly defined shape suggested here. This will give us a basis from which to start studying another question – of the utmost importance in this context – namely what factors determine the outcome of conflict reduction, i.e. which stakeholders will succeed in asserting their claims and to what extent.

The Market

Typical for the establishment of cooperation in a *free market*, for example between the company and its suppliers, is the competition between the various companies on the one hand and the various suppliers on the other. For a precise definition of free competition and for an analysis of a free, competitive market the reader is referred to economics. However, one essential assumption of this theory is that the conditions in which cooperation is to take place cannot be fixed by the individual company or stakeholder (the employer on the labor market, the customer on the product market, the supplier on the market for raw materials or the creditor on the capital market). On the free market the individual company or stakeholder must either accept the conditions of the market or refrain from cooperating. A further assumption is that the conditions are expressed as payments (the market price).

Joint Decision-making

Joint decision-making represents a whole class of institutions for the resolution of conflict. But all its elements have a common characteristic: conflicts are settled and cooperation established by an exchange of information which enables the stakeholders to make a joint decision. This exchange of information may be a joint problem solving, an exchange of factual information or negotiation. These constituents will be discussed in greater detail later. The example of joint decision-making most relevant to our present subject is the establishment of cooperation between a company and a group of employees represented by their trade union.

Coöptation

The term coöptation implies in this context that a stakeholder is represented on the management of an organization. The management group is expanded to provide a stakeholder with a position of some influence within it.

Coöptation is fairly usual. It is quite common for an important customer or a group of customers or suppliers to be represented on the board of a company. Employee representation on the board would be another example.

INSTITUTIONALIZED CONFLICT RESOLUTION – SOME EXAMPLES

It is usual that several institutions for resolving conflict are employed by a company simultaneously on different "fronts". Companies generally establish cooperation with customers and suppliers on a market which is, at least in the main, free. At the same time cooperation with the employees, and to some extent with the local community and the state, is achieved mainly by means of some form of joint decision-making. Creditors on the other hand are sometimes coöptated on to management by representation on the board.

The choice of institution for the resolution of conflict is important. It is also one that management and the stakeholders to some extent can – and at any rate often try to – influence. In the United States it is still possible to find many examples of managements trying to maintain a free market mechanism for establishing cooperation with the employees and avoiding joint decision-making with the trade unions. Counterparts of this situation are presently found in many medium-sized Scandinavian companies who are now considering the advantages and disadvantages of a free market compared with some type of institutionalized cooperation with a big customer or supplier. The debate about employee representation in management can also be seen as the consideration of a choice: which institution would be the most suitable for the resolution of conflict between the employees and the other stakeholders and for establishing cooperation between the employees and the company?

One way in which the various institutions differ from each other is in the amount of freedom bestowed on management. The free market, joint decision-making and coöptation, in that order, can be regarded as stages in a process whereby management gradually cedes a part of its freedom to the stakeholders. As a recompense, greater confidence can be felt about the willingness of the stakeholder to coöperate with the company.

A stakeholder can often exert influence on a company in many different ways. The employees, as individuals, might well have just as much to gain in a free market as they would from joint decision-making between management and the trade union. The Scandinavian system represents a combination of both these mechanisms. The fact that so many channels of influence exist means that the whole network of power-lines along which the claims of the stakeholders collide and are adjusted will be very complicated. Political scientists have acclaimed the value of this, suggesting that it lessens the risk of acute conflict.[1]

[1] It has also been claimed that a common characteristic of the stable democracies is the existence of just such a network in which every individual or group has manifold opportunities of asserting their own interests. This is certainly borne out by most democratic legal systems where the individual is accorded various rights of "appeal".

Political representation based on universal suffrage, which is often regarded as the fundamental of democracy in the Western sense, is a supreme example of an institution for the resolution of conflict. But the model of a company which we presented earlier serves to show why a management cannot simply be elected in the same way as, for example, the parliament and government of a democracy.

If a representative system is to function as a mechanism for resolving conflict in a company, all the stakeholders must be among the electors. This can be practised only in organizations where the same individuals simultaneously play the role of several stakeholders. The main example is the non-profit-making organization whose members are at the same time "workers", "customers", "suppliers" and "owners".

Moreover, the findings of recent research have indicated, without in any way belittling the importance of universal suffrage and general representation, that even in the national sphere the representative system constitutes only one of many ways by which an individual or a group can satisfy their interest in a modern democracy.

EXERTING INFLUENCE THROUGH JOINT DECISION-MAKING

What determines whether or not a stakeholder can make good his claims on the company? Any theory on this subject must naturally be based on certain assumptions about the institutional background – about the methods available for resolving conflicts. Since, from a theoretical point of view, it is the most interesting and the most complicated case, and since it has great relevance to the debate on industrial democracy, we shall examine almost exclusively here the influence that can be exerted by those taking part in the resolution of conflict by means of joint decision-making. The influence of those coöptated will be discussed in the next chapter.

The simple rule of the free market that the buyer must pay the market price to the seller has no counterpart in the process of conflict resolution by joint decision-making. This is difficult to discuss, not only because of its complexity but also because very little theory has been developed on the subject. The tentative theory that will be presented below is mainly based on general decision theory. Its purpose is to investigate the conditions necessary for the conflict resolution process to be successful.

A Model of the Decision-making Process

Most models of decision-making represent attempts to divide the decision-making process into stages. The formal "decision" is included only as the final stage. The following is a typical example:

1. Definition and limitation of the problem
2. Elucidation of goals and boundary restrictions
3. Working out alternative course of action
4. Determining the consequences of these alternatives
5. Evaluating the consequences
6. Comparison of alternatives
7. Decision

(Items 3–6 are bracketed on the page as: problem-solving)

This type of breakdown also lends itself to attempts at describing the problem-solving and decision-making process graphically. An example is the "decision tree" (Fig. 8).

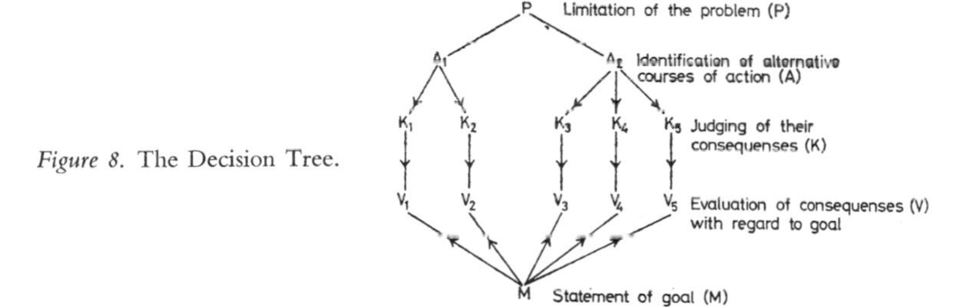

Figure 8. The Decision Tree.

A Complication in Joint Decision-making – Factual Conflicts

Since joint decisions between the stakeholders have to be made against a background of conflicting interests or goals, we could almost say that the natural tendency would be for the parties not to be able to agree. If we look more closely at the decision tree we see, moreover, that other complications may arise. Perhaps an acute conflict breaks out because the decision-makers do not see eye to eye on matters of fact: they disagree about the limitations of the problem and its relation to other problems, or about the action alternatives available or in their interpretation of the possible consequences. This is not the place to analyze in detail the factors which increase or diminish the likelihood of such complications. In practice, it is probably very difficult to differentiate between such *factual conflicts* and the conflicts arising from a clash of interests. In most cases of acute conflict there may well be elements of both.

Treatment of Conflicts

Regardless of whether the obstacle to agreement is different goals or different views of the facts, it is in the interest of both parties to try to overcome the difficulties and to arrive at a joint decision. Both sides therefore start trying either to persuade their opponents or to resolve the conflict in some other way. Usual methods are *exchange of information, joint collection of further information, interpretation, negotiation* and *authoritative prescriptions*. Of these, the subject of authoritative prescription will be left to the next chapter. More space will be given here to negotiation, which is the most important method for resolving conflicts of interest. But first let us take a general look at the other elements in the treatment of conflict.

Exchange of factual information between the parties can reveal the cause of the conflict. If a conflict is purely factual, i.e. arising solely from different interpretations of the situation, then only exchange of information can lead to a solution. A resolution along these lines is often complicated by the fact that the parties differ in their estimate of the reliability of the information. A first step is therefore to collect information jointly, to supplement any already available. It may also be necessary to use new channels of information and, if communication is being hampered by semantic difficulties, to employ some kind of interpreter.

If opposing interests are the main element in the conflict, then negotiation is the most usual method for trying to achieve a resolution. We use negotiation here to mean the exchange of information and the other measures taken by the parties concerned with a view to influencing each other's evaluation of the consequences of the action alternatives. In other words, the purpose of the negotiations is to create a situation in which one party comes to accept the view of the other about the superiority of one of the action alternatives. Threats, promises, analyses of alternative consequences and the discovery of fresh alternatives are all typical elements of negotiation.

Negotiation

The most interesting task for anyone developing a theory of negotiation apart from demonstrating the factors which determine whether, and to what extent, the parties involved in the negotiation can further their own interests, is to indicate the conditions under which negotiations may be unsuccessful as a means of conflict resolution, for instance when an acute conflict arises and, in particular, when sanctions are applied. The first of these tasks is relevant to the debate on industrial democracy because it can illustrate the effect of a particular "democratic" measure – for example, the establishment of joint consultation committees with policy-making powers or of worker representation in management – on the employees' chances of upholding their interests. The second is of interest in so far as there is hope of being able to counteract or prevent strikes or other hostile action.

Some propositions of conflict theory agree fairly well with generally accepted ideas, while others may appear more surprising. Five points will be discussed here.

Access to Rewards

If one party is to be able to uphold his interests in negotiations with another, he must, as a basic prerequisite, have at his disposal something that the other considers desirable. On the other hand, with an abundance of potential rewards in its gift, a party may, in certain situations, find itself in a bad bargaining position. A well known example is the situation of a company running very profitably in favorable times: it may be difficult for management to withstand the employees' demands for an increase in wages.

Economic theory, which regards wages as a market price, gives as the main explanation of this that the company's demand function (i.e. for labor) has changed. In many cases this is of course an important reason which can be included also in a model where wage setting is seen as the result of joint decision-making and negotiation. In this case it will be expressed as a change in management's evaluation of the consequences of alternative courses of action. However, as we shall see below, a theory of negotiation provides some additional explanations.

Access to Sanctions

Sanctions can be regarded as a type of negative reward and much of what can be said about rewards applies also to them. In fact, to refrain from granting a reward – perhaps an increase in wages or promotion to employees or price and delivery or quality benefits to customers – is the most imporant sanction that management has at its disposal. On the other hand, there are circumstances in which sanctions cannot be compared in any way with rewards.

The use of certain sanctions – sabotage, strikes, blacklisting or harmful publicity – is irreversible in a way that a wage increase delayed or a delivery withheld is not. The resulting damage is more or less irreparable. Since the parties involved in the negotiations are assumed to have common interests in at least some respects, the damage will affect both those who apply the sanctions and those against whom they are directed. Strikes and lockouts, for instance, generally harm the employer and the employees. So, if access to practicable sanctions is really to strengthen the bargaining position of one party, the other side has somehow to be persuaded that the threat is genuine.

Related to this problem is the question of whether the sanctions are legitimate. Negotiations between management and stakeholders are bound not only by the rules laid down in a particular company but also by a number of general social norms. Among these are important rules prescribing which sanctions are legitimate and which are not. The circumstances are often rather complicated. A strike is regarded as legitimate in certain situations and illegitimate in others. Nor are the rules always stable. It is therefore important for the party who bases his strength on an access to sanctions, to see that his sanctions are regarded as legitimate. One means is to try to influence public opinion; here great importance will be attached to whether the sanction in question has been used, occasionally at least. A sanction which has not been employed for a very long time gradually comes to be regarded as illegitimate.

What the Parties Know about Each Other

The parties' knowledge of each other plays a very large part in the outcome of the negotiations. The exchange of information is not only a way of solving conflicts on matters of fact but is also an important part of the actual negotiations. We have already given some indication of the importance of keeping quiet about an abundance of rewards and of persuading the other side to believe in your own absolute determination to use sanctions even if they hurt yourself. Many other types of information are equally important and it is interesting to note that it is often as essential to get certain information over to your opponent as it is to receive in formation yourself.

A partly involved in negotiations will probably ask himself some of the following questions: "How much does my opponent know about the alternatives open to him? How highly does he value the rewards that I have to offer and how greatly does he fear the available sanctions? How much does he know about what I think of the rewards and sanctions he has at his disposal? How well informed is he about my views of the consequences of certain measures? How will he make his decision? Will it be an arbitrary one, depending on what mood he is in? What does he know about how I will make my decision? Does he regard me as a completely unpredictable nincompoop or as a rational and systematic opponent?"

Paradoxically, it can often be a great advantage from the bargaining point of view, *not* to know certain things or at any rate to let your opponent believe that you do not. Similarly it can be a great advantage in negotiations *not* to be rational, or at any rate to let your opponent believe that you may not be. This is particularly important in cases where the chief weapon is access to sanctions that are damaging to both parties. Suppose a trade union threatens: "Get rid of the foreman or we strike"; if a strike would damage both company and workers, management's answer will depend largely on whether it believes the threat – on whether it feels "we wouldn't put it past them" or "they're too smart to do anything like that".

The value of information often depends on the situation, e.g. when management demands a wage decrease referring to unfavourable economic conditions, it can be a disadvantage or an advantage for the union to have full knowledge of the facts of situation.

In many cases it is necessary to know something of the opponent's evaluations, before acceptable solutions can be suggested. Without this knowledge it is easily possible to mistake what the conflict is about, producing a situation similar to the factual conflicts discussed above. "Bidding" is one method of exchanging information about the opponents' evaluations. Although the theory on this subject is very sparse, it does at least seem certain that bidding also has effects of another kind, particularly in negotiations between organizations represented by delegates. In such cases, public bidding influences both the delegates and the individual members, probably by means of a process similar to learning.

Social Norms in Negotiation

Social norms exist not only for the procedures of negotiations and the legitimacy of sanctions and rewards, but also for affirming the correct negotiating bids. The concepts of status quo, precedent and compromise are closely related to three norms of this type.

The status-quo norm decrees that if parties who have previously cooperated are to continue to do so, the same conditions shall in the main continue to apply. Any negotiation should be concerned to modify prevailing conditions rather than seek entirely new ones.

The precedent norm purports that if it can be discovered that a similar situation has previously been resolved in a particular way, one side has strong support for the claim that the same conditions shall apply in the present situation. This often seems to be the case even if the conditions are unsuitable from other points of view.

The compromise norm requires that in general a compromise should be sought when conflicting suggestions arise. In other words if one party is to get his opponent to make all the concessions necessary to an agreement he must hold extremely strong cards.

These norms apply to practically all negotiation. But research has shown that in a modern industrialized society there are also special norms indicating the bids which are legitimate between employer and employees in wage negotiations. According to one investigation it is considered legitimate to justify a demand for higher wages by reference to a rise in the cost of living or to recruitment problems in the industry or to the maintenance of the previous wage differential. These norms are quite specific and affect the outcome of the negotiations to a considerable extent. At the same time these norms can probably be greatly influenced themselves in the long run by the action of the parties concerned.

Influence of the Parties' Freedom of Action

One way of avoiding the obligation to compromise, or of killing your opponent's hope that you might compromise, is to render compromise impossible. This may not always be easy, but it is very common that one party tries somehow to burn its boats. The salesman tries to make the customer believe that his instructions leave him no possibility of giving discount. The trade union leader commits himself by public announcements so that the employers will understand that he cannot compromise without losing face. The employers' organization includes an irrevocable clause in its constitution, restricting its freedom of action in a particular sphere[1].

SOME FINAL ADDITIONS TO THE THEORY OF CONFLICT

Formal Conflicts

Cooperation can sometimes break down – and acute conflicts arise – for reasons other than a failure to resolve a conflict of interest. The continuous process of adjustment between individuals and groups, with all that it implies of negotiation, of the promise and bestowal of rewards (payments etc), the threat and execution of sanctions, discussions, analyses, exchange of information and so on, takes place within an institutional framework which, while it may vary in other respects, does always mean that the game follows certain rules.

These rules may be formally prescribed by law, fixed by formal agreement, or simply derived from custom. Like the norms discussed above, they may apply equally to both parties but they may also prescribe differences, making one party responsible for taking the initiative in collecting information, or assigning to the other the formal right of decision. It is then said that the parties are playing different *roles* in the process of conflict resolution.

[1] "An employer applying for or admitted to part-ownership for a certain business is obliged to indicate, at the request of the Board of the Confederation, whether and to what extent he carries on other business activities. At the request of the Board, he is obliged to apply for affiliation with the Confederation also with respect to these other business activities.
In the absence of exemptions specifically granted by the Board, the employer's part-ownership in the Confederation covers all wage and salary earners employed in the business for which affiliation with the Confederation has been affected."

Whether the norms and roles are very formal or less so, extremely complicated or quite simple, each party will have his personal idea of the rules governing his own behavior and certain expectations concerning the behavior of others. When these expectations are not fulfilled – for example, if the employer does not behave during negotiations as an employer ought (in the trade union leader's view) or if the salesman behaves in a way that does not agree with the customer's expectation (as to how a salesman should behave) – the process of conflict resolution may at least temporarily be disturbed. A *formal conflict* arises.

"Unavoidable" and "Unnecessary" Conflicts

We have now introduced three types of conflict: conflicts of interest (resolved or acute), factual conflicts and, finally, formal conflicts. The picture is now sufficiently complete for us to draw an important conclusion concerning the possibility of "abolishing" conflicts.

At the beginning of this chapter we mentioned that modern research tends increasingly to regard the conflict of interest in companies as unavoidable, since no company can entirely satisfy the often opposing claims of its stakeholders. The best one can hope for is that the conflict can be resolved generally by means of some kind of compromise. This apparently pessimistic attitude contrasts sharply with the earlier optimism of industrial psychologists who believed that conflict between employer and employees was simply the result of misunderstanding, personal antagonism, defective negotiating machinery etc.

Now, with a more detailed analysis of the concept of conflict and a classification of types, it is possible to combine the two attitudes. It has in fact been shown that, although conflicts of interest are unavoidable, factual conflicts and formal conflicts can be counteracted and possibly, in an ideal situation, abolished. This is an important conclusion. Before it can be properly understood, it will be necessary to discuss some of the effects of conflict.

Some of the Effects of Conflict

In the introduction to this chapter we stated that conflict, particularly in the debate on industrial democracy, has commonly been regarded as a symptom of social ill. If conflict occurs, it is assumed that there must be something wrong somewhere, either on the part of those involved or in the social system (the company, labor market or society) of which they are a part. It has already been intimated that modern conflict theory does not see things quite so simply.

A conflict of interests can lead to an acute conflict. An acute conflict between two parties means, by definition, a partial or total breakdown in the cooperation between them. But these are not the only effects.

Among the negative features of conflict is the feeling of unease experienced by those involved. It has been clearly and variously confirmed that conflict tends to create aggressiveness and negative attitudes between the parties. This seems to be particularly marked in cases where it is difficult for the opponents to understand each other's motives and one party sees the behavior of the other as a more or less gratuitous attempt to thwart him in the achievement of his own goals.

Conflict may also result in direct damage to the parties concerned or to some third party. Naturally this is most usual in cases where one – or both – parties resorts to the use of sanctions.

These results of conflict are in general well known and need no further detailed presentation. It is perhaps of greater interest to note that modern research has more and more concentrated attention on the functional consequences of conflict. We can look at a few examples. In the case of groups or large organizations, conflict with other groups or organizations often actively encourages loyalty within the group. For instance, a conflict between employer and employees may have the beneficial effect of strengthening and unifying the trade unions (beneficial, that is, if strong trade unions are regarded as desirable). In cases where the conflict of interests leads to an acute conflict this effect seems to be even more marked.

In fact it has been claimed that the division or stratification into groups, be it social classes, organizations, teenage gangs or associations, is chiefly an outcome of conflict. According to this view, conflicts of interest give rise to the grouping of individuals with similar interests who will cooperate with each other against groups with opposing interests.

The traditionally negative attitude towards conflict is probably chiefly directed towards acute conflicts, since these give rise to particularly strong sentiments of displeasure and are generally regarded as costly. Against this view the suggestion has been raised that an acute conflict is usually one stage towards a resolution. An acute conflict can "clear the air", for example by demonstrating the nature of the conflict and perhaps resulting in its treatment and solution. It may for instance be very difficult, perhaps even impossible, for one party to demonstrate convincingly the seriousness of his intent, other than by showing his willingness to suffer the inconvenience involved in the use of sanctions. If the social system is to function in accordance with generally accepted values, this type of acute conflict is probably far less damaging than cooperation based on the crushing superiority of one party.

It is considerably more difficult to judge the value of formal conflicts. Unlike conflicts of interest, they can hardly be regarded as unavoidable. To an outsider they may even appear completely unnecessary. However, they have a definite function in the establishment of institutions and procedures for the resolution of other types of conflict. If these procedures are to be effective, the parties concerned must have the same view of the rules of the game, and although this can be achieved through the prescriptions of a third party (for example the government or an impartial expert or some other mediator), it is probably impossible in many cases to learn the rules of play properly in any way except by playing the game. It is perhaps inevitable that there will be formal conflicts during the first few rounds. It is hardly surprising, for instance, to find that in the early days of the trade union movement many conflicts were concerned with formal matters.

Inevitably, in a dynamic society even the procedures for resolving conflict will sometimes need modification. An excellent example is provided by the relations between company and customers, where the rules about the behavior that is and is not acceptable, seem to be changing almost continuously. And as regards the relations between company and employees, the role of the state in collective bargaining provides a topical example in Scandinavia. It would not be surprising if a change came about in this sphere, not as a result of the investigations of experts but as the outcome of an acute conflict.

Dispelling or Concealing Conflict

It will probably be easier to make a correct evaluation of the methods now available for resolving conflict if, in conclusion, we remind ourselves of some of the existing alternatives. An acute conflict does not after all necessarily lead to a solution. Instead, for example, the conflicting interests may be dispelled or the conflict concealed.

How can conflicting interests be *dispelled*? Perhaps by dissolving the dependency relationship: one party may leave the organization either on his own initiative or as a result of action on the part of management. Much management action is in fact intended to reduce or abolish the company's dependence on a particular stakeholder. Examples are not far to seek. Self-financing makes a company less dependent on external resources. Automation reduces the need for manpower. Diversification of products and markets reduces the dependence on a particular group of customers.

When a conflict is *concealed*, action is taken and the parties concerned think that the conflict has been resolved. In fact it is still there. If, for instance, the intermixture of common and conflicting interests are connected to events which do not occur simultaneously, cooperation may be established at an initial stage, whilst a conflict of interests, immaterial as yet, is concealed by means of an ambiguous agreement which either party can interpret to suit itself. Or management may conceal a conflict by making contradictory agreements, in secret, with each of the parties concerned. Concealment can of course arise purely by mistake: the parties think they are in agreement when actually they are not.

Sometimes conflicts are concealed because society – or even the participants – regard them as illegitimate. It is only too likely that a conflict thus concealed will give rise to others which, although regarded as legitimate, will be more bitter and more difficult to overcome. Thus it has been claimed that wages have often been made the scape-goat for bitter conflict in industries where other nagging dissatisfactions – concerning security, personal relations, job satisfaction – have remained unsolved. As in the case of all hypotheses derived from deep psychology, this is very difficult to confirm.

INDUSTRIAL DEMOCRACY AND CONFLICT RESOLUTION
A SUMMARY

In chapter 1 we presented a basic model of the company and of the interplay between the company and its stakeholders. This we have now supplemented and enlarged. We have shown that the cooperation between different parties concerned in the company exists in a situation where, from many points of view, conflict is normally to be expected. The theory that we have put forward can be summarized as follows (the numbering corresponds with that in Fig. 9).

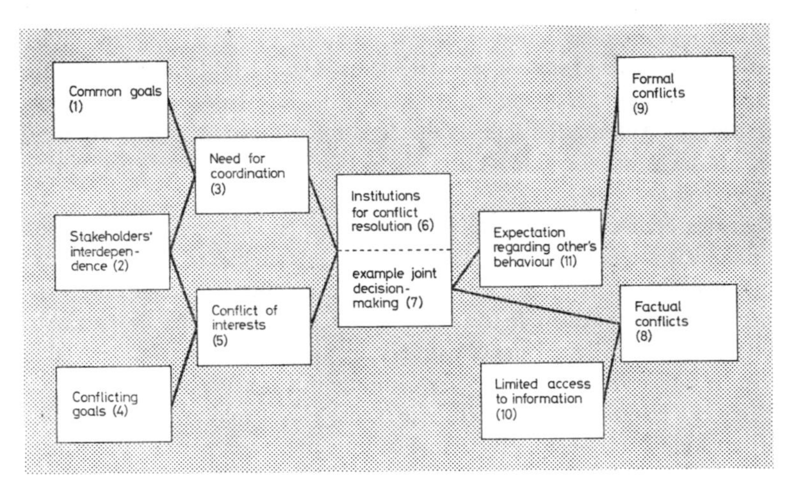

Figure 9. Summary of some important concepts and elements in the theory of conflict between the stakeholders in a company.

The survival of the organization is a common goal of all stakeholders (1). This creates interdependence between the stakeholders (2). Coordination is thus required and often felt to be urgent (3). The stakeholders also have conflicting goals (4) and this often leads to a conflict of interests – usually felt just as strongly (5).

It falls to management to arrange a resolution of these conflicts so that the necessary coordination can be attained. To a great extent the resolution of conflict has been institutionalized. In other words it follows definite rules (6). One of the most important methods for resolving conflicts, and one which has received particular attention in this chapter, is joint decision-making (7).

Taking as our starting point a theory of joint decision-making, we have studied the conditions that determine whether and to what extent the stakeholders can maintain their interests in the company. We pointed out that the joint decision-making can be complicated by other types of conflict, factual conflicts (8) and formal conflicts (9). The first of these arise from lack of information between the parties while the latter occur when the reciprocal expectations of each other's behavior (11) are not fulfilled.

Finally we discussed some of the effects of conflict and came to the conclusion that in the case of several of these it would be an oversimplification to designate them without further ado as harmful. In any case it would usually be preferable to acknowledge the existence of a conflict of interests and to essay a settlement, rather than to dispel the dependent relationship or conceal the conflict.

It seems that a theory of this type is relevant to the debate about industrial democracy on several counts. To begin with, it implies a radical departure from the popular idea that conflict is a sign of social ill health. Instead conflict is regarded as an inevitable consequence of the fact that the claims of the various stakeholders are to a great extent conflicting. Furthermore it has been shown that there are other types of conflict, apart from the "inevitable" ones. As a result, it is possible to indicate more precisely when the "pessimistic" attitude, regarding conflict as something unavoidable, is warranted (conflicts of interest) and when the "optimistic" attitude, which sees conflict as the result of misunderstanding, is justified (factual conflicts and formal conflicts).

Attention has also been directed towards another very important phenomenon, namely the mechanisms for resolving conflicts. The somewhat tentative theory of joint decision-making and negotiation, which has been presented above, throws at least some light on several points that have been much discussed in connection with industrial democracy. Among other things it has been demonstrated that the use of sanctions, regarded by many authorities as something highly deplorable, is an essential and probably inevitable element in the methods of resolving conflict that are available to us at the present time. The theory has also provided some foundation for a discussion of the influence exercised over a company by its stakeholders.

We will return to the practical application of the theory in chapter 7.

CHAPTER 4
EMPLOYEE INFLUENCE AND PARTICIPATION IN MANAGEMENT

INTRODUCTION

Background

In the previous two chapters we discussed the influence of the stakeholders on the goals and policy of a company. We also indicated ways of resolving the inherent conflict between the growing demands of the stakeholders and the need for management to be able to take independent action. In this way we have provided ourselves with some foundation for discussing and analyzing the complicated question of "co-determination", so important to the debate on industrial democracy. "Ought the employees to be given a right in some form to participate in management"? This has been a key question in the Scandinavian debate – in Sweden ever since the Wigforss report of 1923.

This national committee, already mentioned several times above, recommended the introduction of advisory works committees. The trade unions received the suggestion rather coolly and many felt that if the committees were to be at all effective, some sort of right to participate in management would have to be assured by legislation.

The chief source of this and many similar disagreements seems to have been a difference of opinion as to how "much democracy" is really desirable. Naturally enough, some at least of the more radical groups within the labor movement have declared that "co-determination" in some form is essential. On the other hand, groups with a generally negative attitude towards industrial democracy have dismissed participation in management as unthinkable whilst admitting that some other form of influence might be acceptable.

But many have seen an essential difference between measures which grant the workers the clear right to participate in management and those which allow them to wield some influence. Participation, it is felt, would have to be combined with the corresponding responsibility and this, implying as it does a radical change in our present economic system, has been viewed with reserve. Could the employees really take this responsibility? Is not our legislation generally based on their playing a much less responsible role? And since such responsibility would probably fall rather on their organizations than on individual workers, would it fit in with the role of a pressure group organization? This type of argument has clearly lain behind the custom followed in Britain that any leader in a trade union organization has relinquished that position on becoming a member of the board of a nationalized industry. But we also come across cases where the employee organization has accepted some form of participation and some measure of responsibility. The example most frequently quoted is that of the German coal and steel industry, where the workers appoint their own representatives both to the board and to management.

The Classical View of the Problem

The debate about influence versus participation has clearly been decked mainly in the terms of classical organization theory (cf chapter 1, on the traditional view of leadership). The formal rules for decision-making have been observed but no further effort has been made to fathom the actual effects of the right to participation in management. An example of the usual type of analysis is provided by the following:

> The term "employee participation" may refer to certain *bodies* in the company – management committees, the board or the directors, for example – but may equally apply to the different *forms* that exist for bringing influence to bear on decisions. Among these can be distinguished the right to influence, to participation (co-determination) and to decision-making. The right to exert *influence*, prescribed by law or by agreement, implies, in brief, the *opportunity to influence decisions*; but the decision is ultimately made by management. The right to *participation* is the *right to participate in the decision-making*. Such participation or co-determination is obviously found in most governing or executive bodies; it can either be personal in its character or be based on some form of group representation.
> (The Trade Union Movement and Industrial Democracy/Fackföreningsrörelsen och företagsdemokratien/, 1961, pp. 109–110. Our translation.)

The distinction is very reminiscent of the attempted delineation between staff and line in classical organization theory. A "staff position", according to the generally accepted view, implies a position in which influence is wielded by means of advice, whilst a "line position" is invested with the ultimate right of decision. The main concern of the Swedish trade union movement in recent years seems to have been to confirm the influence of the workers rather than to win for them any type of participation in decision-making. It is therefore not surprising that they have hit on the idea of a staff body for employee representation for achieving this. A proposal has been put forward for converting the management committees into staff organs of this type; their function would be to act as adviser to management on particular questions. In this way the management committee would be on an equal footing with other committees in the company (cf Fig. 10).

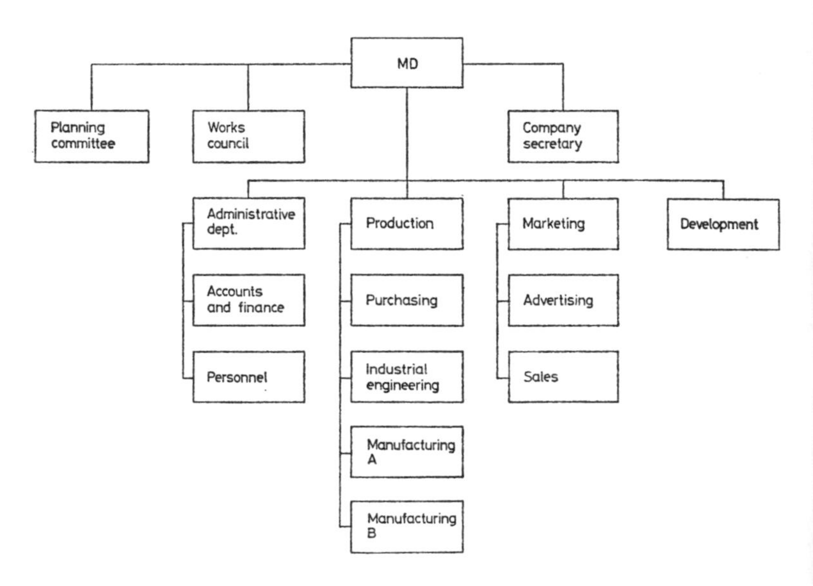

Figure 10. An example of how a management committee can be placed in the organization chart of a company.

The Aim and Contents of the Chapter

Traditional studies of influence and participation in management have thus been limited in their scope: they have said very little about the consequences of the various measures possible – of, for example, a changeover from influence to participation. Some debaters have pointed out that, to judge from experience, some forms of influence can actually involve greater power over decisions than the formal right of decision. But little else has been said.

In this chapter we shall therefore first examine the difference between influence and participation according to our theory. We will then investigate the consequences of a changeover from influence to participation. We shall continue to limit ourselves mainly to those rather vaguely defined decision areas earlier designated as the goals, policies and plans of the company.

If we are also to discuss the possible effects of participation, there is one respect in which our theory is incomplete. In many people's opinion the chief distinction between the various types of influence and the right to participation concerns the kind of authority that obtains. In the last part of the chapter we shall therefore define the concept of authority and examine the various factors that affect it.

THE MEANING AND EFFECTS OF INFLUENCE

Briefly, chapters 2 and 3 lead to the following conclusions: all the stakeholders in a company have some influence on goals, policy and plans; the basis of this influence is the mutual dependence of the company and the stakeholders. Before we can examine the question of whether a stakeholder can make good his claims on the company, we will have to study the mechanism for resolving the conflicts that inevitably arise from the frequent clashes between such claims. If, for instance, a conflict is to be settled by means of joint decision-making, various important factors will affect both parties' chances of satisfying their claims: their access to rewards and sanctions, their access to information about each other, their freedom of action and what they believe to be their counterpart's freedom of action and, lastly, certain social norms concerning negotiation. Thus the concept of influence has been related here to a theory of the interplay between a company and its stakeholders. We shall now try to define and analyze the concept of participation in the same way.

An Ambiguous Concept

One definition, already quoted, describes the right to participation as the right to take part in making decisions. This definition probably agrees with common usage. If we reformulate it in the terms applied in the previous chapter, the *right to participation* becomes a formally prescribed rule of joint decision-making.

However, in view of our findings concerning the decision-making process, even this definition cannot provide us with an unambiguous concept of participation; on the contrary, participation can mean very different things, depending on the amount of commitment envisaged at the different stages of the decision-process. Many people "take part in the decision-making", from the man who introduces the problem, to those who influence the goals governing the decision, from the one who can suggest or evaluate alternative courses of action or in any other way contribute to the problem-solving process in the light of his experience, knowledge or imagination to the man who formally decides on the final choice of alternatives.

It can of course be argued that employees demanding the right to participate are not interested in the whole complicated decision process but, chiefly, in the final, formal decision. That may be so. Later, however, we shall see that this argument perhaps misjudges the significance of such limited participation. And in any case it is possible to take part in the final decision in many different ways and with varying consequences, according to the situation.

For the sake of clarity we shall assume here that, in the debate on industrial democracy, the demand for participation refers to all phases of the decision process. Participation in the final formal decision only can then be regarded as a special case.

Before examining the consequences of the right to participation, it is important to remember that decision-making in a company is often split into various parts entrusted to a wide range of individuals and groups. It has thus been accepted in the main that decision-making is far too complicated for a single person. Consequently, the right to participation will require much of those who possess it. This difficulty, too, we shall ignore for the sake of simplicity and assume that the employees have the formal right to partake in decision-making in the company by means of their representatives (cf Fig. 8). The interesting point then is to see how this will affect their chances of exercizing influence and satisfying their claims. We can conveniently divide the decision-making process into four stages:

I. Taking the initiative
II. Formulating the goals and norms
III. Problem-solving
IV. Making the final decision

Participation I – Taking the Initiative

The questions which could be the subject of problem-solving and decision-making in a company are, theoretically, countless. As examples of subsidiary spheres within which, even in quite small companies, there are always almost unlimited opportunities for initiative can be mentioned: investments, personnel administration, industrial engineering, introduction of new products, savings campaigns, improvement of planning methods, revision of routines, reorganization and so on. It has already been mentioned that in this situation "management-by-exception" means that in general nothing is done if it can be avoided. Even in companies which look beyond the acute problems and try to plan for longer periods, it is nevertheless the same basic mechanism which governs the sifting of problems. Long-range planning is really, in the main, an attempt to foresee in good time the problems which will sooner or later have to be tackled.

Certain questions, then, are regarded as urgent. How are these recognized? We have already indicated an answer; initiative is taken when it is needed to avert threats to the survival and stability of the organization. The organization is defended chiefly on two fronts: by means of direct action intended to maintain good relations with the stakeholders and by measures intended to maintain or improve efficiency. Indeed, efficiency is one of the essential requirements for retaining the stakeholders in the company.

Thus, regardless of whether or not they have the formal right to participation, the stakeholders – including the employees – do have opportunities for influencing the first stage of decision-making when the questions that require handling are determined. Their influence at this stage is naturally indirect, in that it is based on the claims made on the company by the employees or their organizations in their role as stakeholders. Unfortunately there are no empirical studies to help us here; it is impossible to say anything definite about the extent of the influence that employees can have on the choice of initiative. But one thing is clear: many writers on the subject find the influence already too great.

> "They (many managements) have left the initiative to the union. They have usually not even known what to expect in the way of union demands. ... When first told that certain union demands are about to be made, the typical management refuses to listen. ... Then, when the demand is made, management tends to turn it down as "impossible" and as "certain to ruin the business", if not our free enterprise system. Three days to three years later management caves in, accepts the demand, and in a joint statement with the union leader hails the agreement as a "milestone in democratic labor relations".
> (Drucker, 1954, p. 83)

It is easy to criticize a situation like this; indeed the writer quoted above closes his remarks with the exclamation: "This is not management, it is abdication". But if we take as our startingpoint the theory developed in chapter 2 about company goals, it does not seem so iniquitous to claim that in many cases it is quite natural that initiative comes from the employees. The claims of the employees and other stakeholders will generally be the driving force behind initiatives. Various factors – the size of the company and its organization, the nature of the question and so on – will determine who will perceive the need for initiative. In large companies it is becoming increasingly common to employ specialists, responsible to a top staff manager, to act as expert "initiators". Possible ways of giving employees a greater chance of taking the initiative themselves will be discussed later.

Participation II – Formulating the Goals and Norms

As regards stage two in the decision-making process, the formulation of goals and norms, it has already been suggested in some detail in chapter 2 that the employees are among the stakeholders who exert considerable influence. It was also pointed out that it is generally the responsibility of management to balance the claims of the stakeholders and interpret the possibilities inherent in the situation.

This means that employees often have a "negative" rather than a "positive" influence; it is easier for them to make their claims in such a way that a particular goal is excluded or to introduce prohibitions, rather than to make constructive suggestions, setting goals and norms for action. Participation, in some form or other, would mean a considerable change in this respect. But we must not forget that formulating goals, norms and plans, after balancing the claims of the stakeholders and interpreting the possibilities of the situation, is a highly specialized task requiring qualified experts.

It is possible that the right to participation may make it easier for a stakeholder to uphold his claims during the process of formulating goals. Apart from anything else, if communication between management and this particular stakeholder has previously been inadequate, the stakeholder will now have a chance to bring his claims out into the open. Or he may find he has access to additional sanctions or to better information about management's standing in the negotiations.

Participation III – Problem-solving

The third stage in the decision-making process – the discovery of alternative courses of action and the analysis and evaluation of their consequences – is generally a task for qualified experts, at any rate when the problems are at all complicated.

When facing this type of task, most managements are probably somewhat worried about available resources and ready to welcome any suggestion which seems to offer something constructive. Nevertheless, only rarely has the participation of elected representatives of the employees been regarded as a likely aid. Instead, it has been more usual to enrol experts in special research groups, to use outside consultants etc.

It has to be admitted that such measures are generally just about as far removed as possible from common ideas of industrial democracy. And, since at least the unskilled employees are not specialists, it also seems clear that any exaggerated optimism about their chances of contributing to the problem-solving would probably be doomed to disappointment. Nevertheless, the workers are not entirely without influence. In the search for good ideas and for the knowledge with which to assess them, it is quite usual for the specialist, in the normal course of his work, to provide the ordinary worker with the chance to help, if it is felt that he might have something of value to contribute. Work study experts, office efficiency experts and other specialists will usually interview the workers concerned as a regular part of their investigations. Any changes suggested are generally brought up for discussion. A savings campaign will be so presented as to engage the interest of the workers. In other words, at any rate in large companies with highly developed staff departments, there already exists a channel other than the normal one between boss and subordinate, along which suggestions and ideas from the employees can flow and where, indeed, such contributions are systematically encouraged and collected.

Participation in the problem-solving process does not necessarily involve improved opportunities for the furthering of personal interests. But there is always the possibility that the specialists might use – or at least be suspected of using – his strong position to impede unnecessarily the interests of another party. If the employees were able to partake in the problem-solving, albeit somewhat passively, they would perhaps be able to exert some sort of control on possible abuse of technical know-how.

Without denying that such cooperation on the part of a stakeholder might be valuable, we will simply point out here that management itself generally tries to insure against any partisanship on the part of its specialists. One of its major weapons is akin to the type of joint decision-making that we discussed above. There we studied joint decision-making as a stage in the resolution of conflict between a company and its stakeholders, now we see an example of the same mechanism at work within the company, its purpose being to utilize the varied knowledge of the specialists and to provide a vehicle for mutual control. In this way the company is assured of a factual and impartial treatment of the problems under consideration.

Participation IV – Making the Final Decision

The final, formal decision, as an element in the decision-making process, has been the object of much misunderstanding, partly because it is often difficult to isolate it from the problem-solving stage and the formal decision-making. However, if we bear in mind the complex nature of problem-solving it can be seen that the final act of "making the decision" is often of rather slight importance. When one alternative stands out as obviously superior and fully acceptable in view of the given goals and of the information available, the final decision is little more than a matter of form. It is only when a decision has to be made in a very uncertain situation, or when the goals are vague and perhaps conflicting, that the final right of decision is of major significance. In such a case there is a considerable amount of what is usually called in decision theory the "absorption of uncertainty".

Those partaking in the absorption of uncertainty have an opportunity – in the same way as those involved in problem-solving – of concealing partiality behind a façade of knowledge. But, most important, participation in the final decision involves, according to generally accepted social norms, also responsibility for the decision.
The relation between responsibility and the right of decision is a complicated one, of which space allows only a brief discussion here. The view that responsibility necessarily accompanies the right of decision is a reflection of several social norms. One of these holds that nobody should absorb uncertainty who will not be affected, at least to some extent, by the consequences of a bad decision. Another norm brands it as illegitimate to make demands which cannot be satisfied on account of decisions previously made by oneself. Another asserts that anyone who has participated in the formal decision is bound to cooperate loyally in carrying it out.
Thus responsibility for the decision and for its consequences will do much to prevent those concerned from unduly pushing their own interests, for instance in connection with the formulation of goals and norms. There is sometimes even a conscious attempt on the part of management to gag a stakeholder by giving him a part in the right of decision.
One of the chief methods of giving stakeholders responsibility is by means of coöptation (see chapter 3), that is, by involving representatives of the stakeholders in the company management. Researchers have designated this as one of the most effective methods of defending an organization against an aggressive and powerful stakeholder.
The various relations between the right to participation and a stakeholder's chances of furthering his own interests in the company are

summarized in Fig. 11. This shows, admittedly, that on several counts the right to participation may open the way to greater influence, but there are also several reasons for its doing just the opposite. The risk of losing influence is maybe even greater than the chance of gaining it, particularly if very great weight is given to the social norms that link participation to responsibility. Perhaps the main conclusion to be drawn from our brief analysis is that there is much need for an empirical investigation starting from partly new bases.

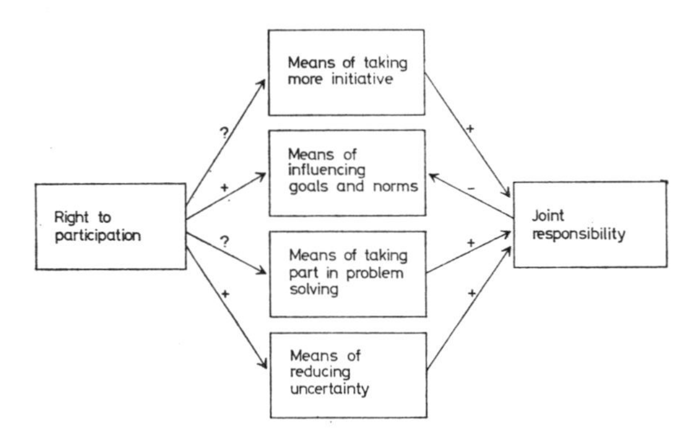

Figure 11. Some relations which can exist, in a particular situation between a stakeholder's right to participation and his chances of protecting his own interests.

PARTICIPATION AND AUTHORITY

To recapitulate: we have now seen how difficult it is to demonstrate any fixed relation between an increase in formal participation and an increase in actual influence without further amplification of every particular case. Perhaps the reader will be of the opinion that our analysis is in any case incomplete, since we have made no mention of any other effects that may follow a changeover to participation; of the fact, for instance, that it will involve a radical change in the social relationship between the employees and their representatives on the one hand and management on the other and that this may have desirable effects of its own. Those who argue along these lines will probably not find the theory suggested in chapters 2 and 3, in which the interplay between stakeholders and management is seen as a series of negotiations, as relevant for the discussion of employee participation. Emphasis is more likely to be given to the importance of providing the workers' representatives with more authority in the company.

Management, too, ascribes great importance to authority and to the acceptance of authority. Most top executives and other managers would probably agree that an organization simply cannot function without a system of authority. In explaining defects in an organization, expressions such as "unclear authority", "insufficient authority", "lack of authority" are often heard.

If a foreman, a department manager or a top executive is asked how he thinks that a particular person gets authority he will almost always answer: "Authority is delegated from management". The precepts of classical organization theory thus predominate. But simple examples show that the idea of authority as something coming from "above" is, to say the least, incomplete. The doctor wields authority in relation to his patient. The subordinate can behave authoritatively towards his boss.

Nor is the concept of authority entirely uniform in scientific literature. In the main, two views have predominated. Sociologists and political scientists have been inclined to see authority as "institutionalized power", that is, the type of power attached to a particular position in a social system and made legitimate by the official norms. Another trend has been to regard authority not as a characteristic of one person, but as a characteristic of a social relationship between two persons, growing out of the interplay and intercourse between them. Starting from our earlier discussion of decision-making and influence, we will show how the two viewpoints can be made to coincide.

A Theory of Authority

As a basis for our discussion let us take the following definition of *authority*: Authority is a characteristic of a social relationship between two individuals: A is said to be in authority in his relation to B, if B unquestioningly accepts a directive from A as a basis for his decision-making or his behavior.

The authority can be derived from either of two sources. It can be based on power, or on an acceptance of mutual goals combined with superior access to information or knowledge on the part of the authoritative party. One possibility is thus that B accepts a directive from A as authoritative because he expects that A will employ sanctions against him if he does not obey it. This ability to apply sanctions (or offer rewards) is what is meant here by power. In an organization, this power is based to a great extent on the reciprocal claims of the organization and the stakeholders (cf chapter 2). The power of the organization over its members derives mainly from its ability to satisfy or frustrate the claims that the members make upon it. However, social norms permit the use of certain sanctions and rewards such as wage increases, promotion, dismissal etc, and inhibit the use of others. Formally delegated authority depends on the right to apply certain of those that are regarded as legitimate.

Alternatively A can have authority in relation to B, if B believes that they both have more or less the same goals and, furthermore, that A has access to more reliable information or greater knowledge. He therefore regards the directive from A as authoritative and accepts it without question as a suitable way of achieving the common goals.

Superficially the grouping into two types of authority may show certain similarities with the distinction so often made in administrative literature between line and staff authority. According to the classical theory, the line manager's authority is based on his formal position and his power while the authority of the staff specialist depends on his superior knowledge. But the line manager's authority can also be based on the recognition by his subordinates that he is striving for their good (and that of the organization) and on their admission that his position provides him with a "better grasp of the situation". And, vice versa, the authority of the staff specialist can be based on the power he wields as personal adviser to a high-ranking line manager, or on the influence he exercises on wage setting and promotion (probably in the personnel department) etc.

It is characteristic of the authoritative relationships in an organization that they are often comparatively stable and are included as part of the role system. Instead of referring to the existence of power or of common goals and superior knowledge in every case, the organization develops certain standards as an important part of its stable pattern of behavior, for example that subordinates accept the authority of their superiors on particular questions. The little addition "on particular questions" is, however, very important. All authoritative relationships are limited to apply to certain questions or spheres and are, moreover, often restricted to a certain period of time.

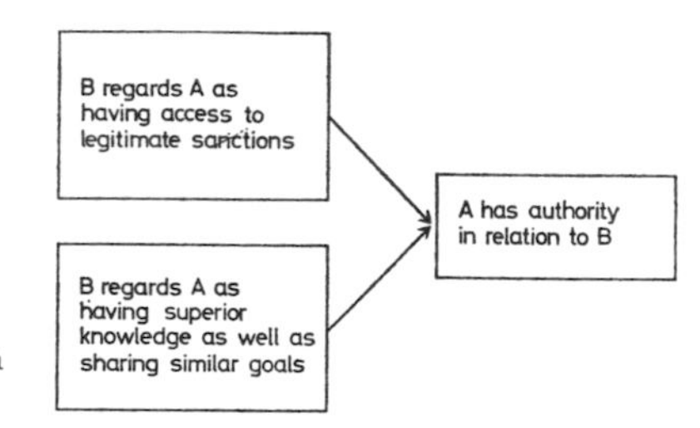

Figure 12. Authority can be based on power or knowledge.

The system of authority in an organization is always highly complicated. Its form will depend not only on the formal organization but also, for instance, on the informal group formations, the channels of communication, the personal characteristics of the organization members – in particular their knowledge – and on a number of other factors.
The development of the system of authority as a part of the social role system, or rather as one aspect of it, runs parallel to – and is modified by – the actual exercise of authority. The "stock" of authority can thus be consumed or added to.

The Right to Participation – Status – Authority

What, then, according to the theory developed above, is the relation between the formal right of decision and authority? For example, how will the authority of the workers' representatives on the management committee be affected by the fact that the committee is granted a certain right of decision and the workers themselves a formal right to participate in decision-making?
In Fig. 13 we have demonstrated some of the most important relations which can be expected to play a part. Before we comment on these, a brief discussion of a concept appearing in this diagram – status – would not be out of place.
By an individual's *status* is usually meant a relative measure of his pondus. Sometimes a distinction is made between the status which accompanies a

particular position or role and the personal *prestige* of a person or a group. A ranking-list or – as is more common in modern companies – a job evaluation system provides a scale for measuring status.
Obviously it is very difficult to differentiate between personal prestige and the status attached to a role, since these tend to react upon one another. A management committee consisting solely of persons of low prestige will tend to have low status as a committee.
In fact it is one of the most characteristic features of status that it is dependent on so many factors. It is particularly important to note that there is a relation between the status attaching to all the different roles that one person fulfills. This means, among other things, that there is a relation between the status relations in a company and those in the society or the culture of which the company forms a part.
The status system has many consequences. Some of these are of great positive importance to the organization and to the individuals concerned. To persons or groups having high status – for example the various managers and executives – is, rightly or wrongly, ascribed access to all kinds of sanctions and superior characteristics, such as greater knowledge. From the individual's point of view this is important, because it permits him to accept the authority of a person of high status without loss of self respect. From the point of view of the organization it is valuable that the status system provides support for the managers.

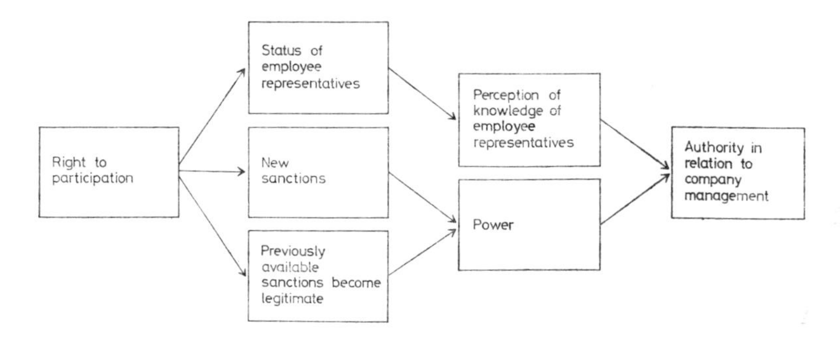

Figure 13. Relations between the formal right to participate in decision-making and the authority of the workers' representatives vis-à-vis management.

At the same time the status system is a part of the system of rewards. One of the claims made by the employees is that the organization shall give them status.

Fig. 13 illustrates that we expect the right to participation to increase the status of the workers' representatives. From what has been said above, however, it appears that several other factors are also significant, for example the prestige enjoyed by the individuals concerned. There is generally a positive relation between social status and the distribution of coveted benefits and advantages. This is probably no simple, causal relationship but rather an example of mutual influence between, for example, status and remuneration. If membership of the management committee involves personal benefits, it can be expected that the status of the members will increase. Another important factor is certainly the importance of matters handled by the committee.

To recapitulate: increasing the status of the workers' representatives means that, rightly or wrongly, they are ascribed power, superior knowledge and access to better information. This gives them greater authority. Furthermore, their authority can be expected to increase as a result of improved opportunities for recruiting qualified committee members.

In so far as the right to participate in decision-making is combined with access to new sanctions on the part of the workers, or if sanctions already available are made legitimate, the authority of their representatives will also be strengthened. It is important to remember in this context that the usual aggressive types of action, such as strikes, are not the only sanctions experienced by management as effective; the publication of criticism, the aggravation of relations with the workers or the lowering of the company's reputation in employer circles or other similar measures can be equally powerful.

Other Ways of Influencing the Authority of the Workers' Representatives

Thus Fig. 13 shows that a formal right to participation can be expected to contribute to an increase in the authority of the employees' representatives. At the same time it also reveals something else, namely the complicated nature of the relations which determine the authority of an individual or a group. For instance, just as a boss can destroy by his behavior the authority that the formal delegation of sanctions has bestowed upon him, so can the workers' representatives nullify the authority which accompanies a formal right to participation. Incompetence on the part of the members, a tendency to promote the unilateral interest of a group or a party, vacillation and unwillingness to take responsibility for the decisions once made, are examples of characteristics and behavior which can destroy the formally assigned authority.

A tendency in the opposite direction is also possible: it is quite possible for representatives on the management committees to create considerable authority without possessing any right to participate in decision-making. Fig. 14 illustrates some examples of important relations which could be used to build up systematically the workers' authority, for example in the management committees.

If the members are regarded as truly representing the employees and as being in a position to influence employee attitudes, it will be recognized that they have at their disposal very considerable sanctions. This type of management committee member has considerable power and can behave authoritatively. Manifest support from the workers' organizations also means power and, thus, authority.

If superior knowledge is to bestow authority, it is important that those concerned have the same goals. If the workers' representatives on the management committee are to be able to behave with authority based on knowledge, it is essential that they be regarded by others as loyal to the committee and to the company. Otherwise management will always suspect that the information put before them is prejudiced and that it is being utilized solely to uphold the interests of the employees. Confidence in the individual representatives and favorable experience from cooperation with the management committees are the most important prerequisites for belief in the loyality of the representatives.

Something can probably even be achieved if the members of the committee try to decide jointly what the goals of the company really are. If they succeed, they will have a common frame of reference which, whilst it may be open to different interpretations, can nevertheless facilitate creating reciprocal loyalty.

The type of information to which the workers' representatives can lay special claim will probably concern employee attitudes and, to a lesser extent, local working conditions. To achieve this, a vague general knowledge will not suffice: considerable activity will be required of the workers' organizations and perhaps the establishment of special systems for making opinion-polls, measuring attitudes and gathering information in other ways among the "electors".

SUMMARY

We have now concluded the theoretical analysis of several questions which, in one way or another, affect the balance of interests in a company. In chapter 2 we developed a basic theory of the interplay between a company and its stakeholders and outlined a general picture of the role of management in the company. Part of chapter 3 was devoted to a more detailed examination of the ways in which conflicts between stakeholders can be resolved, this being one of management's most important tasks and closely related to the various aspects of employee influence. Discussion of these questions continued into the present chapter.

If workers' representatives are perceived as being (or having).

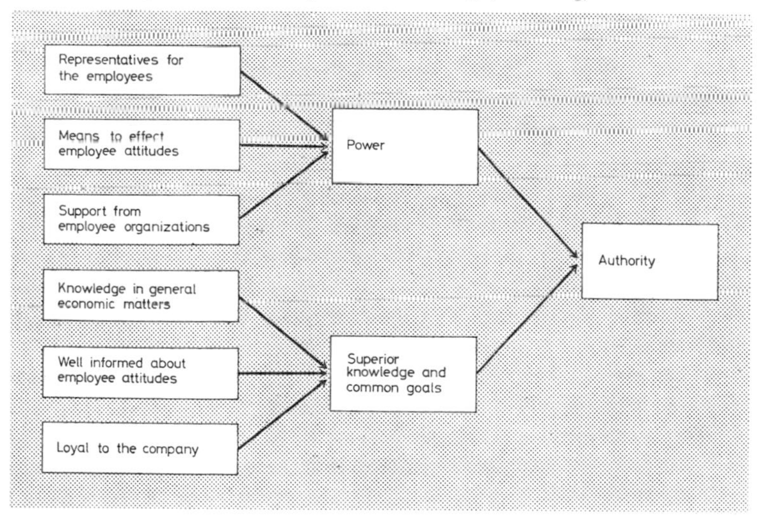

Figure 14. Diagrammatic summary of some ways of increasing the authority of the workers' representatives, for instance in a management committee, vis-à-vis management.

After briefly summarizing the classical approach and presenting a general model of the various stages in the decision-making process, we tried to analyze whether, and to what extent, employee influence is increased by participation. The result was somewhat inconclusive. It is of course difficult to make a general statement, but it seems that in many situations there is considerable risk that the right to participation would lower the employees' chances of satisfying their own interests in the company.

To supplement this picture and, above all, to clarify another concept frequently employed in the debate on industrial democracy, we concluded the present chapter with an analysis of the relation between the right to participation and authority. It appeared, among other things, that a certain type of participation – for instance, through a management committee endowed with the right of decision – would probably increase both the status and the authority of the workers' representatives. At the same time it was pointed out that this result can also be achieved in other ways.

In chapter 7 we shall again apply our theory to a more detailed examination of the balance of interests, the resolution of conflict and the influence and authority of the workers. First, however, the theory needs some amplification and, with this in mind, we will now turn to some questions centering on the efficiency and productivity of the company.

CHAPTER 5
PARTICIPATION, JOB SATISFACTION, PRODUCTIVITY

Hopes and Expectations

We have previously discussed two very ambitious goals of industrial democracy: to find the best way of protecting the rights and interests of the workers and to avoid industrial conflict, widely regarded as one of the most serious ills of society. We can now turn to the highly relevant, related problems of job satisfaction, personal adjustment and productivity. It has, expressly or tacitly, been assumed that the increased satisfaction and improved personal relations expected to flow from participation would lead naturally to the coveted rise in productivity.
This argument was well put by Hjalmar Branting, the first socialist prime minister in Sweden, when commissioning the 1923 study of industrial democracy:

"Industrial democracy thus appears as a complement to the efforts of the trade unions to protect the interests of their members; but at the same time its very structure links the workers more closely to production, creating a new spur to increased productivity which is in the interests of the community as a whole. Insofar as the worker on the factory floor and in the office can follow the management of the company as it were from inside, and exert some influence on its development and progress, he is liberated from the paralyzing sensation of being no more than an inanimate and indifferent cog in a vast machine, with which he has little or nothing in common. In such a system, even as a part of large-scale production, he has better opportunities than before of gaining satisfaction from his work".
(The Problems of Industrial Democracy 1923. /Den industriella demokratins problem./ (Our translation).

In the idiom of the industrial sociologists, we might say that more participation and exchange of information increases motivation and, consequently, productivity (cf Fig. 15).

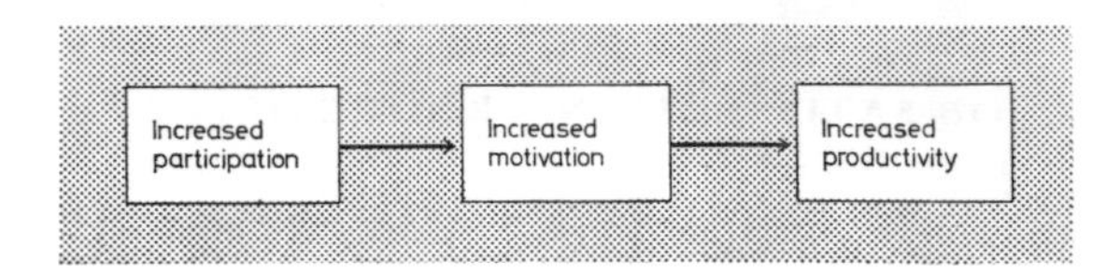

Figure 15. One of the mechanisms by means of which participation is expected to lead to an increase in production.

It is also plausible that participation or employee influence may spark off other mechanisms leading to a rise in productivity. For instance, participation might result in greater exploitation of the workers' experience and knowledge. Or, by giving employees more influence it might at least be possible to limit the opposition to necessary changes (cf Fig. 16). But we must not forget that many have never ceased to question whether any connection can be taken for granted between participation, employee attitudes and productivity. Naturally we find this doubt mainly among those who are sceptical or critical in their general attitude towards the practical program of industrial democracy. Those who support an expansion of democracy in working life but who have been influenced by this type of counter-argument, or those whom experience has taught to be sceptical of the most optimistic assumptions, have generally reacted in one of two ways. Either they have decided, consciously or unconsciously, that one must go all out for satisfaction or for productivity, but not for both simultaneously. Or they have hoped that the conflict will prove to be fictitious, that the apparently irreconcilable will somehow accord. One quotation from the Swedish debate can serve to illustrate the type of discussion that is usual:

"National and international competition have forced up demands for productivity. But the principles and values concerning the conditions and the dignity of man, which are the cornerstones of a democratic society, imply among other things the assumption that continuously high productivity can be achieved only when men are well adjusted to the circumstances of their working life. However, the opposite view is sometimes expressed ... There is no foundation for assuming any conflict here ... Nevertheless we have every reason to note and answer such views. They spotlight the question – irrelevant as it may be in this context – of the conflict between the demands of technology and productivity on the one hand and our democratic values on the other. Whenever a real conflict exists between them, let there be no doubt about our attitude. It must be resolved in favor of the latter".
(Man at Work /Människan i arbetet/ 1961, pp. 2 f. Our translation).

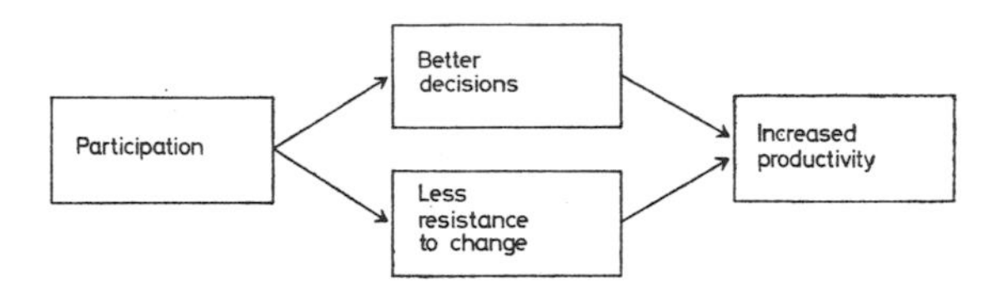

Figure 16. Two more examples of the expectations expressed, directly or indirectly, about the effect of participation on productivity.

Although this discussion has recently been decked in modern sociological or psychological terms, we should remember that the problem is as old as the history of industrial democracy itself. When workers' councils were introduced during the First World War, what was the aim? Chiefly to encourage hard work, increase productivity and help to win the war. The new wave of interest in industrial democracy which appeared during the Second World War and the subsequent period of full or over-full employment, was due partly to a similar impetus.

As we will show, this program of industrial democracy received much support from a trend in social science, often described as the human relations movement, which can most simply be summarized by the slogan "industrial democracy is good for the company". In this chapter we shall examine the program and the results of this movement, later proceeding to a survey of some other impulses in psychological and sociological research which can increase our understanding of the relation between participation, job satisfaction and productivity.

RESEARCH – AN INTRODUCTORY SURVEY

Scientific Management and Human Relations

Scientific interest in the influence of psychological factors on working conditions has a relatively long history. Most of the pioneers of the scientific management movement were interested in the systematic analysis and organization of work as a means of stimulating productivity. Taylor made some simple observations on the psychology of the wage system and emphasized the importance of the systematic selection of staff. But that was about the limit of his interest in psychology (cf Fig. 17). However, some of his colleagues and disciples had an eye for finer shadings and devoted much attention to the people who were to do the work. It was thus not long before the psychologist came to be regarded as one of the many specialists in the scientific management team.

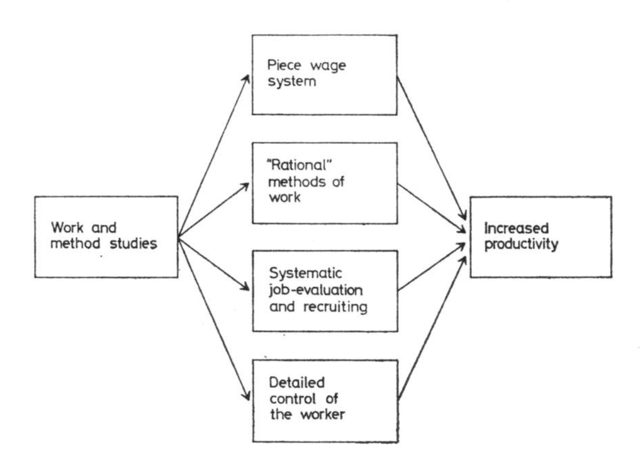

Figure 17. The aim of the scientific management movement was to increase productivity. By means of "scientific" studies of working methods it was hoped to provide a basis for a just piece-wage system, for placing "the right man in the right place" and for regulating and controlling work in greater detail. All this would lead to an increase in productivity.

Research in industrial psychology was at first closely related to the views of the pioneers of scientific management and was directed mainly towards two tasks: to develop methods for personnel selection and to throw light on the problems of fatigue. The latter proved to be much more difficult than had been expected. In particular it was difficult to isolate physical tiredness from psychological fatigue.

Studies at Western Electric, which have become widely known, provided something of a link between modern industrial psychology and some of the previously rather unsuccessful research into the problem of fatigue. The aim of the investigation was originally to try to find the optimum working conditions. A series of experiments was initiated in which such factors in the working environment as lighting, ventilation, rest pauses etc were varied. From the surprising observation that productivity increased more or less regardless of how these factors were altered, attention was turned to various social conditions in the environment. It was pointed out that the working group seemed to play an important part and that loyalty to the group, group norms, the status of the group members and similar factors were all significant.

Research concerned with the work group, enriched by impulses from Freudian psychology and may other sources, began to be seen as a sharp contrast to the studies of the scientific management movement. To some extent this was justified. The supporters of the human relations movement have often severely criticized the industrial engineers working in the traditions of scientific management for "unscientific" methods and for presenting an over-simplified mechanical model of "man", in contrast to their own methods and theories with roots in social psychology, sociology and social anthropology. To put it briefly, the chief characteristic of the human relations theories is the assumption that social organization affects productivity, perhaps more than any other single factor.

From the very beginning, much interest was devoted to what was usually called morale. "Morale" was measured in various ways, either directly in terms of absence from work, personnel turnover etc, or indirectly by assessing attitudes to work or to the company. Morale, too, was thought to be strongly related to the social organization and its correlation with productivity was assumed as a matter of course (cf Fig. 18).

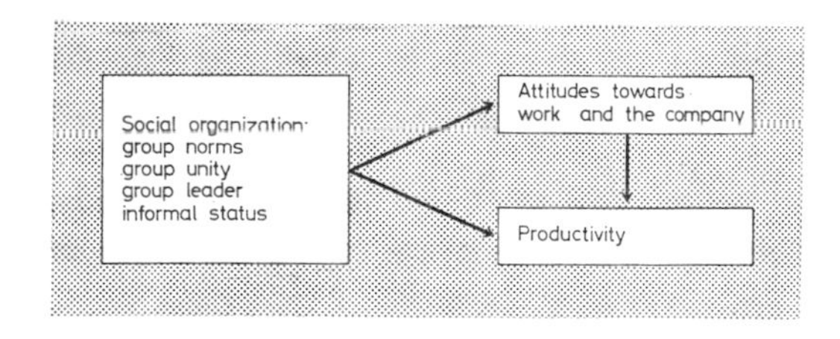

Figure 18. Some basic themes in early industrial sociology.

Recently, however, scientists have maintained with increasing emphasis that the scientific management and the human relations movement are not really so different from each other after all. For example: both accepted practically without question that the formal organization of companies, as they found it, was immutable; both have even been accused of partisanship in the interests of management. To take Mayo as an example, his starting point was in fact the problem, as experienced by management, of increasing productivity. One critic uses hard words, claiming that in this way researchers

> "uncritically adopt industry's own conception of workers as *means* to be manipulated or adjusted to impersonal ends. The belief in man as an end in himself has been ground under by the machine, and the social science of the factory researchers is not a science of man, but a cowsociology".
>
> (Bell, 1947, p. 34).

In recent years an increasing number of voices have been heard to declare that even the human relations movement has failed from a scientific point of view. Its methods have come to be criticized in much the same way as its supporters once criticized the scientific management specialists, namely for unjustified, exaggerated simplifications and an unscientific approach. The basic assumptions have been declared erroneous and the preliminary results untenable.

However, these views should not be exaggeraged. Lewin, Mayo and their followers have had an enormous influence both on the general lines of thought and on the development of particular methods. Their empirical results have also much greater tenability than many of the more far-reaching interpretations that others have sought to impose upon them. Nor can it be denied that the human relations movement has influenced industrial management, particularly perhaps the views and methods of the personnel specialists. A striking example is the great importance allotted nowadays to keeping employees informed. We are today unlikely to find a management calling itself "modern" or "progressive", who would not admit the importance of this. The trade unions, on the other hand, have by and large remained sceptical and suspicious – at least according to some research reports.

Recent Research

In most respects recent developments have been somewhat disparate and therefore difficult to summarize. With some simplification, however, we can discern a few main trends.

To begin with, a large group of researchers have concentrated their efforts on problems of leadership, by trying to understand the conditions necessary for the successful leadership of people at work, often with the express or implied purpose of finding out whether the interests of the individual and those of the organization can be made to harmonize.

Within this group, two major schools can be identified. One, in the spirit of the human relations movement, has directed its attention to the problems of the supervisor or foreman. The other has studied general problems of management and administration, examining the whole question of how the organization exercises influence on the behavior of its members. If one can judge purely by the volume of published results, the latter group were slower to get started, but during the last ten years has more than made up any lee-way.

A third school – unfortunately very divided – has made some attempt to return to the questions that interested the scientific management movement. Its followers feel that a basic weakness in all studies of leadership, has been the exaggerated interest in psychological and social environment and the neglect of work and technical conditions as important factors affecting job satisfaction and productivity.

Although it is difficult to judge, it seems probable that the last two of these lines of research are the most likely to succeed. Lacking a basic theory about the way in which organizations influence their members, studies of specific leadership problems will always run the risk of superficiality and error. Whereas the possession of such a theory should make it easier to broaden the scope of the research and prevent too narrow an interest in the problems and behavior of the foreman.

In view of these considerations, this chapter will be devoted first to a rather brief report of some results from traditional leadership research, followed by a review of other research in which technology has been included as part of the environment to be studied. Finally we shall try to relate some of the results of this research to our earlier survey of company goals, thereby introducing into our discussion the concept of productivity and its measurement. In the next chapter we shall look at leadership from the point of view of modern administrative theory.

As researchers became interested in social organization as an essential factor influencing morale and productivity, it was natural that they also took note of the conditions affecting it. The Western Electric studies turned the searchlight on supervision. The leader, especially the supervisor or foreman, came to be regarded as the most important link between the formal organization and the social conditions in the working group (cf Fig. 19).

In popular literature, and in general discussion of the subject, it has often been claimed that the successful leader can be recognized by certain personality traits, and his behavior by certain easily identifiable characteristics. For a long time assumptions of this sort guided most research. Attempts were made to pin down the typical characteristics of the leader by means of psychological tests and other methods of evaluation. Typical of these studies is the great variety of "essential" characteristics suggested. However, traits suggested by one writer often run contrary to those apparently observed by others.

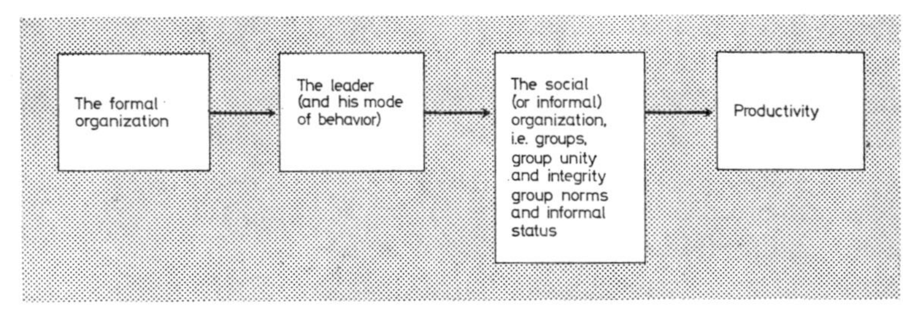

Figure 19. A basic theme in industrial psychology has been that the leader influences productivity through his influence on the social organization.

In later research there has instead been a tendency to characterize the relation between the leader and the led as the main factor contributing to successful leadership. A number of circumstances have been regarded as inter-related, together forming a leadership style. One style has been described, with slightly varying content, as "democratic" or "participative". The behavior of a democratic leader has generally been characterized by an interest in the subordinates as people and not only in their work, by willingness to consult and give plentiful information rather than to issue orders and control all activities. The "authoritarian" style of leadership has been presented in contrast to this and has been characterized by roughly the opposite traits: restrictive control down to every detail, too little interest in the subordinates and excessive interest in results, a paucity of information and strict orders rather than consultation. The democratic leadership style, with the support of certain general psychological theories, was assumed to be superior to the authoritarian. Some of the results of earlier research seemed to confirm this, but later results have often seemed to prove the opposite; there is considerably more doubt now than there was fifteen or twenty years ago about the possibility of formulating any general rules. Thus the hunt for the best leadership style has largely proved just as unsuccessful as the earlier search for the best type of leader.

A major obstacle in most of these studies has been the problem of measuring the "success" of leadership. Indirect measures, such as the loyalty of the subordinates, attitudes to work, job satisfaction or sense of group unity have often been used as measures of effectiveness. But, strangely enough, results have frequently shown that although the democratic leadership style preached by the human relations movement may be "successful" according to one or more of these criteria, it does not necessarily react favorably on productivity. And even in most cases where

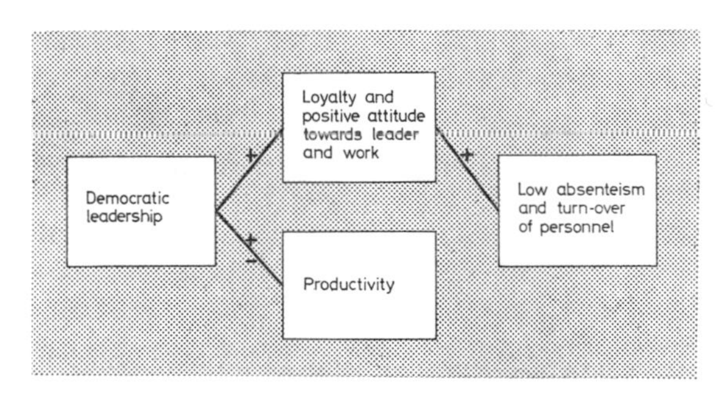

Figure 20. A democratic style of leadership generally seems to lead to greater loyalty on the part of the subordinates but, in the main, seems to lead as often to lower as to higher productivity.

democratic leadership seems to have had a beneficial effect on one or more of the criteria used, the differences in results between the democratic and the authoritarian style of leadership have been small.

Most researchers have thus come to the conclusion that more factors will have to be introduced into the analysis if clearer results are to be obtained. Various factors have been suggested. To begin with, attempts have been made to get away from the clear-cut division into "democratic" and "authoritarian" and to draw finer distinctions. Some authors claim that this has been done successfully. A well-known book, recently published, opens as follows:

> "Managers with the best records of performance in American business and government are in the process of pointing the way to an appreciably more effective system of management than now exists. With the assistance of social science research, it is now possible to state a generalized theory of organization based on the management practices of these highest producers". (Likert, 1961, p. 1)

By this, the writer means, that the various tendencies will be found more often among successful and efficient managers than among the less successful. Another writer has summed up these characteristics as follows:

1. To demand self control and apply general rather than close supervision.
2. To be "employee-centered" rather than "job-centered".
3. To provide clear objectives but leave employees greater freedom to arrange their work according to their own judgment.
4. Instill high goals without resorting to authoritarian pressure.
5. To create an organization of which coordination is a cornerstone.
6. To increase influence and power at every level in the company so that even the lowest rank and file members do not feel entirely powerless.
7. To support the employees and the company – not the company only – and to be firm and just in so doing.
8. To keep the organization members better informed and not to conceal information.
9. To be interested in the experience and ideas of the employees, to seek such information and make an effort to utilize it to the full.
10. To use group decision techniques and approach problem-solving through the group.

(From: Zaar, 1962, p 24) (Our translation).

Different factors have been suggested by others: for example, the reputation of the boss for being more knowledgeable than the subordinates, his keeping a certain distance between himself and them, his reputation as a consistent, reasonable person etc.
A critical examination of the various suggestions and of the theories called upon to support them, can only lead to the conclusion that, empirically, most of them have rather loose foundations.
As a result of this latter observation, many students of this subject have drawn the conclusion that not only must the description of possible leadership styles be extended; it must also be accepted that leadership situations vary considerably. It has been claimed, for instance, that a particular group may be more suited than another to a particular style of leadership; a particular leader may be more suited than another to lead in a particular way; the general social climate may partly determine which leadership style will be successful; the type of problem that a group will have to face may decide how its leader must behave in order to achieve success. The resulting complexity of the whole question will be examined in the next chapter.

TECHNOLOGY AND JOB SATISFACTION

The results of some recent research in this field have aroused interest in technology's positive or negative role in creating social conditions of a kind that will promote job satisfaction, facilitate easy adjustment and lead to good relations.
We all know that the work in some industries is dirtier and in some cases more difficult than in others. It has also been recognized that on a wide, international scale, the dockworkers – to take one example – have been involved in a great number of strikes while the clothing industry – to take another – has a good reputation for more or less unbroken industrial peace. It is hardly likely that this can be explained by any world-wide tendency for one industry to have more skilful trade union leaders and employer representatives than another. Nor can economic factors, varied as they are, wholly explain the phenomenon. A decisive answer to this and similar questions has not yet been made, but it has been noted that in the industries with a history of numerous strikes the work is uniform and the workers generally live near each other in closed communities. Cor-

respondingly, in the industries known for their peaceful development, the work is varied and the workers live, dispersed, in relatively open communities where opportunities of contact with workers in other industries are many.

One writer has studied the attitudes and behavior of management and supervisors and compared the situation in the process industries, the mass producing industries and the unit producing industries[1] and makes the following summary of her results:

"In firms at the extremes of the scale (the process industries and the unit producing industries), relationships were on the whole better than in the middle ranges (the mass producing industries). Pressure on people at all levels of the industrial hierarchy seemed to build up as technology advanced, became heaviest in assembly-line production and then relaxed, so reducing personal conflicts ... The production system seemed more important in determining the quality of human relations than did the numbers employed". (Woodward, 1958, p. 18)

It has been suggested that the chief cause of this may be that in the unit producing industries it is so extremely difficult to achieve detailed control that no-one has succeeded in finding a method. In the mass production industries the situation is different:

"In large-batch and mass production, continuous efforts to push back the limitations of production put considerable pressure on employees. Targets were set progressively higher, incentives of many different kinds were offered, and production tended to proceed by drives. But in the last resort the pace was still set by the amount of effort the operators were prepared to put into the job". (Ibid., p. 29)

When we go further along the scale towards total mechanization and come to the process industries, the exercise of control is so mechanical and exact that pressure on the workers can once more be reduced to a minimum. Productivity in a process industry is only indirectly dependent on the efforts of the man at the machine; the machine rather than the foreman will exert control.

"Most of those interviewed seemed to resent authority less when exercised over them by the process than by a superior". (Ibid., p. 29)

Other studies – for instance of companies where work has been arranged along a production line – have shown similar results. The foreman, no

[1] By this is meant here industries whose production is mainly geared to customers' orders, i.e. shipbuilding, bespoke tailoring, atomic reactor construction, etc.

longer having to check the rate of work, has come rather to play the role of teacher, helper and adviser. Relations between foreman and workers have thereupon immediately improved. These results should not be misconstrued nor given too broad an interpretation: the attitude to work, for instance, has not always improved simultaneously. On the contrary, the "mechanical" control exercised by the production line has caused dissatisfaction and even aggression towards the company.

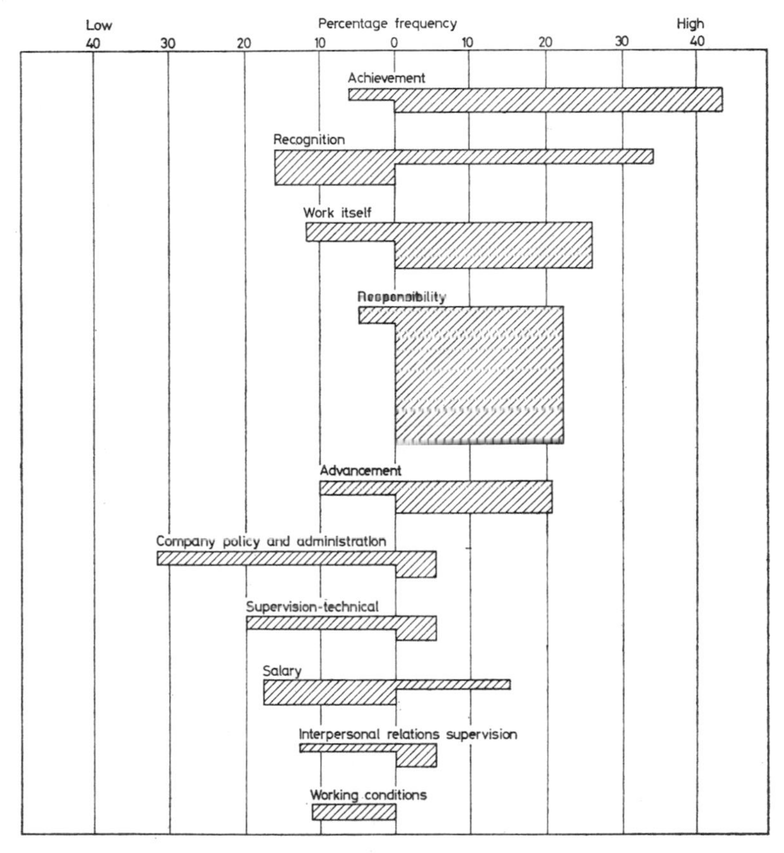

Figure 21. In a study of two hundred salaried employees a comparison has been made between factors that have contributed to marked satisfaction or dissatisfaction.

The effect of automation on job satisfaction has been the subject of considerable study, but results have not been unanimous. It could have been expected, for instance, that automation would lead to a general increase in the difficulty of the work and to greater variety. But even on this point expectations have not been fulfilled in all cases. It has been reported from a semi-automated steel works that the unskilled work decreased, but so did the skilled work – just as much if not more. Relations between workers and supervisors sometimes improved after automation but, again, sometimes they did not. As an explanation of the latter cases, it has been suggested that the big costs involved in a standstill compel management to exercise harder pressure on the employees.

As will be seen from these examples, the usual assumption has been that technology affects job satisfaction because it changes the system of leadership and the relations between leader and led. There are some researchers, on the other hand, who have emphasized that technology influences the work itself and thus has a more direct influence on job satisfaction.

In one investigation the factors affecting employee attitudes to work have been studied by investigating "critical incidence". Each person was asked to tell about the period in his life when he had experienced very strong feelings of satisfaction or dissatisfaction. The interviewer tried to discover which factors had contributed to these feelings. Some of the results, which have been confirmed in other studies, are summarized in Fig. 21. They show, among other things, that the work itself and the circumstances directly connected with it (for example, responsibility and opportunities for promotion) were very important in determining job satisfaction.

CHANGING THE WHOLE WORKING ENVIRONMENT

Leadership has thus given rise to a rich flora of studies and theories. In contrast the influence of technology on social conditions and job satisfaction is a subject of which we have very little and incomplete knowledge. In psychological and sociological research, technology has usually been regarded as a given factor. Experiments have been made with job-rotation and job-enlargement – sometimes on quite a grand scale – but they have generally taken place under the auspices of managers and have been regarded as technical experiments rather than psychological or sociological.

If we should hazard a forecast of the future direction of research, we must note some experiments initiated by the Tavistock Institute. Their aim is to change the socio-technical system with a view – among other things – to increasing the opportunities for contributions from the employees. One of the most interesting experiments involves a combination of self-government and job rotation. This has been tried in a British coal-mine, and in an Indian textile mill; similar experiments have been started by an Anglo-Norwegian research group in two companies in Norway. So far results are said to show that at least in certain situations it is possible to increase job satisfaction and productivity simultaneously by such means. The leader of the first experiments recounts:

> "In one coal-face unit recently studied by my colleagues and myself ... a team of 41 miners undertook the responsibility of providing for the manning of the works groups on each of three shifts of just under eight hours. As a group, they accepted complete responsibility for this in such a way that there would be sharing between group members of jobs with different degrees of satisfaction and difficulty. Since the groups were on a single collective payment agreement no questions arose over differential rates of pay. In developing their systems of rotating members from shift to shift the initial interest of the group was to avoid the unfairness of a man being tied for a prolonged period – or even permanently – to an unpopular night or afternoon shift; they especially wished each to have an equal share of the "good" day shift.
>
> ...
>
> Later on, within each sub group of 20, there developed a further system not of shift but of job rotation. Flexibility was provided within a basic pattern, and certain crucial jobs were shared amongst those best suited to them. This acceptance of responsibility for self-regulation of shift and job rotation has persisted throughout the life of this particular coal-face – over two years at the present time". (Clegg, 1960, p. 121 f).

The theory behind several of the experiments has been borrowed from Freudian psychology and is rather difficult to summarize briefly. One basic proposition holds that it should be possible to adapt methods of work and leadership so that the new "sociotechnical system" thereby created satisfies the traditional demand for efficiency at least as successfully as the former and the psychological and social demands of the employees more so. The following are instances of the hypotheses employed: there is an optimal variation of work, tasks can be combined in meaningful patterns, workers should have the possibility of formulating the goals and standards of their work, all work should require some problem-solving, every worker should be able to see his contribution to the final product, workers who are dependent on each other should work close to each other, etc.

CRITICISM OF THE PRODUCTIVITY CONCEPT

One conclusion that we can draw from the research as summarized above is that the relationship between working conditions, job satisfaction and productivity is much more complicated than was originally thought. Another indication of this comes from researchers who find that a basic fault in earlier research lies in the methods of measuring productivity and even in the actual definition of productivity itself.

It has been claimed, for example, that if it proves difficult – as we have seen that it does – to find a simple correlation between a democratic leadership style and productivity, this may partly depend on the fact that productivity is measured over too short a period. It has been suggested that whilst a decline in the attitude towards superiors, work etc might be counteracted temporarily by, for example, harder pressure on the employees, in the long run this is not possible. Although these considerations should be regarded more as a hypothesis, or even a pious hope, rather than a scientifically confirmed proposition, they are nevertheless very disturbing methodologically. It is obviously both difficult and costly to extend investigations of this type over periods long enough to include the long-term effects. Moreover in lengthy experiments it is practically impossible to prevent changes of other types from interfering uncontrollably with the investigation.

Objections to the productivity concept have been of two kinds. Since productivity has generally been expressed as output (volume or value of production) per input (of different production factors, labour among others), critics have been able to attack both the measurements of "output" and the measures of "input".

Criticism of the output measurement has been directed mainly at the narrow interest in products. After all, the company is not solely concerned with producing goods and services. It is also a place of work; job saticfaction is therefore a goal in itself and can be regarded as one of the outputs.

Those who criticize traditional methods of measuring the input of production factors have pointed out, among other things, that an hour's

work may range from the extremely demanding to the relatively effortless and that the only correct measure of input must somehow determine the amount of effort required of the worker. The effort will be both physical and mental. It is therefore by no means certain that "easier" work requires less effort or that a shorter working day is less tiring.
A more comprehensive productivity concept could be defined as "satisfied needs per input", both terms being understood in a broader sense than usual. These views, although put forward by scientists of repute, have not yet been used as the basis for any empirical studies but only in general discussion.
It does not seem too far-fetched to see a connection between the question of the productivity concept and the discussion in chapters 2 and 3 about stakeholders' demands and the goals of the company. It is not altogether improbable that economical and social developments have now advanced to such a stage that the relative power and influence of the stakeholders, and the claims that they make, have changed so much that many long accepted ideas must be abandoned. We have shown, for example, that the worker nowadays is a stakeholder of considerable influence. It is quite likely that he is now prepared gradually to reformulate his claims, giving greater weight to the demand for job satisfaction. According to our present theory this will find expression in the goals of the company; consequently there seems every reason to take up the concept of productivity and its measurement for reappraisal.

CONCLUSIONS

Research into leadership styles has not provided any simple answers to the questions posed. The hope that a democratic style would prove unquestionably best has not been fulfilled. Nor has the hope of finding simple relations between job satisfaction and productivity in the traditional sense.
But although researchers are less ready nowadays than they were a few decades ago to give clear and simple answers to the questions we should like to put to them, something very important has nevertheless been achieved. We have been forced to realize that the environment which affects performance and job satisfaction is composed of many and varied conditions. Among these must be counted all those aspects that so inter-

ested the pioneers of the scientific management movement – the organization of work and such physical environmental factors as temperature, lighting, noise and ventilation. Just as important, however, are the factors emphasized in the human relations movement, chiefly perhaps the social relations in the working group. Finally, we must also include working methods and technology in its broader sense, embracing the whole of the production and administrative system of the company.

Faced by this complex situation it seems best to start more or less from the beginning, if we are to try to develop a more satisfying theory. The significance of this for one of the questions discussed here – the analysis of leadership – will be shown in the next chapter.

CHAPTER 6

LEADERSHIP – A NEW APPROACH

INTRODUCTION

Although the problems of leadership have been the subject of extensive research, results have so far been meager. Ardent disciples of "industrial democracy" have perhaps been particularly disappointed since it has always seemed to them that a democratic leadership style must be the best way of harmonizing the interests of the individuals and the organization. But it has not been possible to confirm even this.

We have already suggested reasons why the relative failure of past research is hardly surprising. Leadership is a complex concept, hard to define; leadership situations vary almost unendingly. The type of propositions suggested have just not been adequate.

Another limitation of many leadership studies is that they have been concerned almost exclusively with "front line leadership" – mainly with the foreman on the factory floor and, less often, with the office supervisor. This is understandable since the further up the hierarchy we go, the more difficult it is to measure the effectiveness of leadership, or to clarify the demands that the leader's situation places on him.

This concentration on the "front line" has had serious consequences, including a kind of tacit assumption that the most difficult problems in an organization are caused by faults among the foremen. More recent research has shown, however, that leadership problems are probably just as important higher up in the hierarchy, and that the behavior of the higher managers has great influence on that of the leaders further down.

Up to now the debate on industrial democracy has also concentrated on leadership problems at the lower levels. At the same time, however, the situation in industry and other organizations has been changing. Technical and administrative development has been rapid and all-embracing;

the corps of white-collar workers and of various technical experts has grown enormously. It seems likely that this is where we will find most of the future problems of industrial democracy.

There has for some years now been much debate on the effects of information technology on management practices. Much of what has been said is relevant to our present subject. It has been pointed out that, previously, the trend in many companies was towards decentralization. It was thus hoped to make better use of lower managers by giving them greater powers. Now, chiefly as a result of developments in automatic data processing, this tendency seems to have been reversed. With the help of new technical equipment, management can collect and process a wide range of information very quickly; decisions can be made by central experts probably more efficiently than by local managers. It seems likely that middle management will lose ground both quantitatively and qualitatively. The organization of the future will no longer resemble a pyramid, as of old, but rather a football balanced on a box.

This type of prophesy has met with some opposition, but cannot be wholly ignored. Even if it proves only partly true, it will certainly aggravate the problems discussed here.

In any event it seems clear that no thorough analysis of leadership problems can be restricted to the supervisory function of the foreman in the workshop. In the following pages, using models and viewpoints from organization theory, we will try to clarify the concept of leadership, having in mind leadership *at all levels in in an organization*. We shall examine different forms of leadership, different leadership styles and possible measures of effectiveness. Such a broad approach naturally has its complications but seems necessary after the failure of earlier attempts with a limited analysis.

LEADERSHIP IN ORGANIZATIONS – THE TRADITIONAL VIEW

The usual view of leadership in organizations stems directly from traditional administration and organization theory. The basic assumption is that the goals of the company are given and that the task of management is to steer the organization towards them. In particular this involves the coordination made necessary by specialization. In most attempts to describe this function of management, the usual frame of reference is the hierarchy modelled on the organization chart. This envisages a structure consisting of units of working groups, each headed by its own boss. The groups are arranged in a hierarchy of successively larger departments, these too headed by a manager. The managers in the pyramid are connected by "lines" or channels for the transmission of orders and reports (cf Fig. 22).

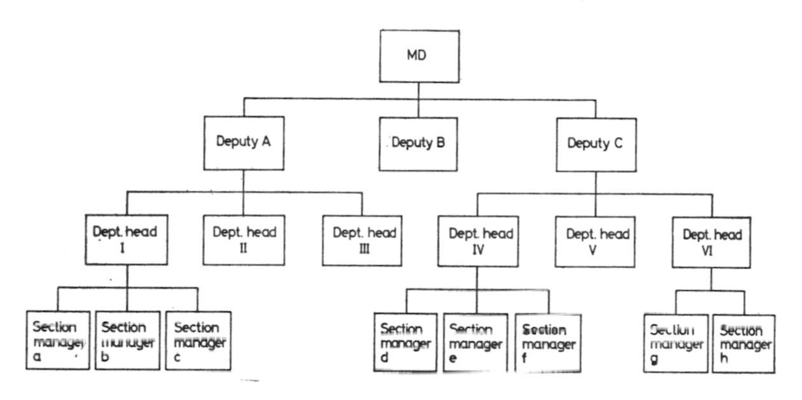

Figure 22. The traditional organization chart illustrates the hierarchy of managers, providing the answer to the question "Who is whose boss?"

With the help of this model the theorist of the old school then describes how the organization functions with the help of two "leadership mechanisms". The first mechanism is the formal delegation of work, responsibility and authority from the president down through the various levels of management. One of the purposes of this is to provide the managers with the powers necessary for putting into practice the second mechanism, namely "briefing". Orders, too, follow the "line" from boss to subordinate, down through all levels.

This simple model of the organization and of leadership has deep roots in Western culture. In Christian doctrine we continually come across the idea of power and authority "in the highest" from whence all rights proceed down to the other levels in a pyramidal hierarchy. Linguistically the same conception is revealed by terms such as "superior" and "subordinate", "high" position and "low" position, to start "at the bottom" and

to climb "up". Anyone familiar with organization charts will recognize the phenomenon and will know, for instance, how important to the employee is the distance from his "own little box up to the top".
Since its conception this model has been modified, mainly in two ways.

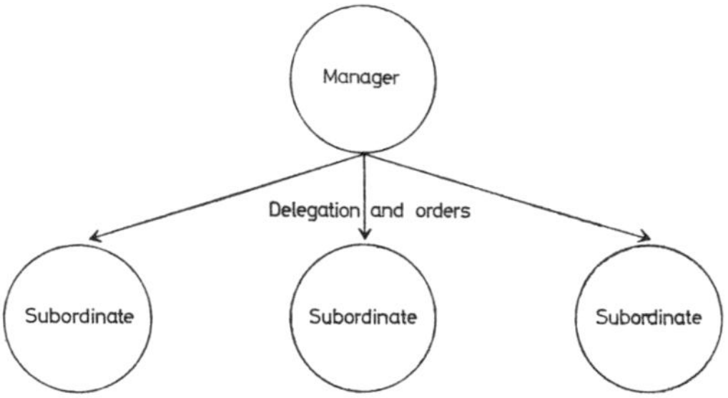

Figure 23. According to the traditional view of how an organization functions, the subordinate is controlled by delegation and orders from the boss.

Manager
Delegation and orders
Subordinate
Subordinate
Subordinate

The first tries to recognize the growing influence of a rich flora of specialists. The second has been inspired by sociological studies of working groups. Both these developments have been mentioned briefly in previous chapters; they will now be examined from a rather new angle.
Modern companies employ a great many highly qualified functionaries who have no position as managers in the "line". These "staff" functionaries wield great influence over other units, thus quite clearly exercising some of the functions of leadership. In order to find a suitable formula for the work of the staff, the classical theory has been modified by the "line-staff principle", which admits that staff may give advice and instructions. But it is still claimed that the delegation of work, responsibility, authority and the right to give orders can flow only from the boss and down the normal "line".
The other important modification is connected with the concept of informal or social organization. This concept has a long history in sociology but became topical mainly as a result of the studies in the Western Electric company (see chapter 5 p (77)). In these studies the social grouping of the workers emerged as a very important factor affecting productivity. It was found that informal groups wield great influence by authorizing certain behavior norms and appointing "informal" leaders. It was also shown that in some cases the main function of these norms and leaders is

to oppose the norms prescribed by management and its representatives and in general to obstruct the work of the formally appointed foremen and supervisors. Consequently the informal organization is often regarded as something of a competitor of the formal set up.

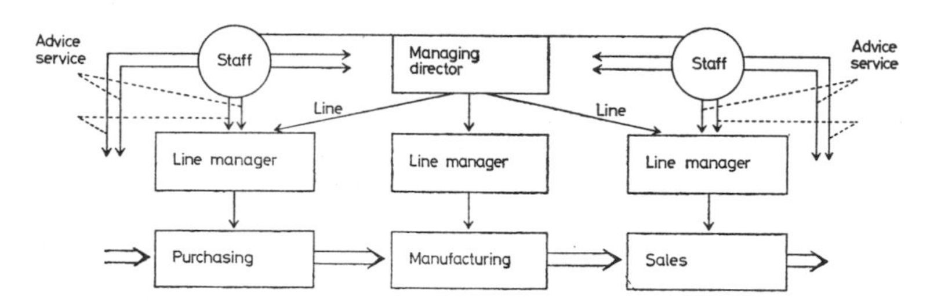

Figure 24. The "line-staff model" is a modification of the traditional organization model. Control is exercised not only by means of orders from the line manager but also through advice from staff specialists.

Neither of the two modifications outlined above, however, has essentially altered the classical view of how management functions in a company. The organization chart can still represent the general view.

The traditional view of leadership has had a number of consequences, of which the following three are particularly worth noting:

1. "The leader" and "leadership" become more or less synonymous. Since each leader is responsible for one part of the organization, the study of leadership becomes in fact the study of leaders.
2. The role of the leader is supposed to be homogeneous and clearly defined. It therefore seems natural to seek "the most efficient leadership style".
3. Influence and the formal right of decision are regarded as almost identical concepts; adequate formal authority is the most important prerequisite of efficient leadership.

LEADERSHIP IN ORGANIZATION – A NEW APPROACH

It is sometimes claimed that social and political problems are often the result of linguistic confusion. Particularly risky is the tendency to group every set of phenomena into a simple dichotomy. It is generally accepted that language governs perception; the linguistic classifications will therefore give rise to a similar perception of reality. The terms "leader" and "led" are examples of this confusion: the simple designations seem to have been accompanied by a widely cherished belief that they correspond to recognizable, homogeneous groups in real life. An important feature of the approach to leadership presented here is the questionings of this belief.

Recent research indicates, in fact, that in many respects the classical views of leadership were far too narrow. Three points may be made:

1. Leadership has many more functions than the classical theory allows. In different situations the importance of these functions and the demands on the leadership will also be different.
2. Leadership can be exercised in many ways other than by delegation and "briefing".
3. Every organization member is controlled by impulses from many different sources: he himself often has some control over many others apart from his direct subordinates.

These points represent a considerable shift in the view of organizations and leadership. It should perhaps be mentioned that this is not the result only of modern research; there are also various technical and administrative developments which have essentially altered the way in which the company of today functions as compared with its precursors of only a few decades ago. Changes outside the companies have also had their effects. Many of these developments are fairly obvious and have already been discussed. Nevertheless we want to focus the attention on some of the more important here.

One feature that distinguishes most modern corporations from the large organizations of the past, such as armies and churches, is the much greater dependence between units and individuals. This creates a need for "horizontal" contacts. Empirical studies have shown this need to be particularly urgent in dynamic environments where companies have to adjust continuously to new conditions.

But perhaps the most important changes are linked to technological development, which results in extensive specialization in almost all companies. Specialization, moreover, does not affect production only; the leadership function is equally affected as the number of specialists involved continues to grow. Many leadership tasks can nowadays be

executed only be means of cooperation between several persons or groups.
At the same time social and economic changes in society have brought the authoritarian leadership style into disrepute, so that it is often regarded as unsuitable and sometimes as downright unacceptable. This attitude can be found among both superiors and subordinates.
Lastly we can note that because many modern companies have to function in rapidly changing environments, their most important problem may no longer be to achieve efficiency in existing conditions but to be able to adjust to new ones.
It is easy to see that these developments, and the more complex view of leadership, will have important consequences for the debate on industrial democracy. But we should perhaps wait to draw any conclusions until the complex nature of leadership has been further studied.

LEADERSHIP FUNCTIONS

The classical theorists regarded the company's goal as a given factor. We have seen that this view is unrealistic. Instead it is probably management's most important task to formulate goals that are adapted to the opportunities offered by the company's situation, goals that will satisfy the demands of the stakeholders. Although this broader concept of the leadership function refers chiefly to top management, the theory can also be applied to smaller units in the organization, i.e. working groups or departments. Units appear, flower and die, just as companies do. A new working group or department starts, expands, declines and disappears. And in this smaller world, too, successful leadership will involve adjusting to new situations, exploiting the available opportunities and satisfying the demands of the stakeholders. The individual organizational unit has its own special group of stakeholders and these include in the first place the company as a whole, the employees of the unit and its leader (cf Fig. 25). At the same time the leader must strive to retain the members in the group. The distribution of the "rewards" that he has at his disposal – for example wages, status symbols, coveted tasks, praise – is an important leadership task. A certain limited turnover of personnel may be regarded as desirable; too many losses would be a threat to the existence of the unit. But it is not enough simply to retain the employees in the group:

members must also be encouraged to make the greatest possible effort. The distribution of rewards and the motivation of group members are two leadership functions which partly, but not entirely, overlap.

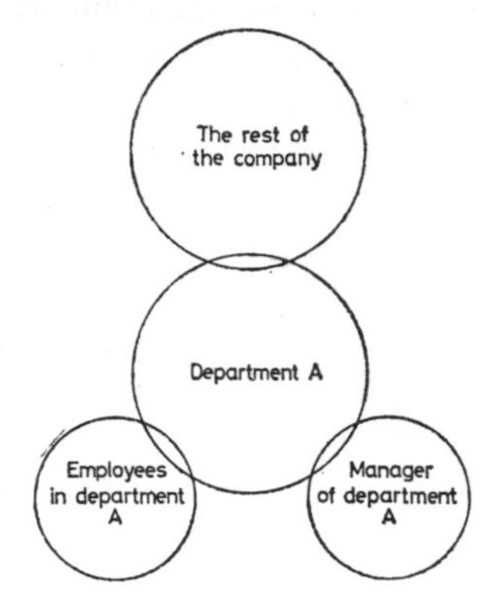

Figure 25. The stockholders of an organizational unit, i.e. the individuals and groups who make claims on it and on whom it depends, consist, among others, of the employees of the unit, its manager and the rest of the company.

But leadership does not begin and end with the job of defending the unit, large or small, against threatening inner collapse; the leader must also be on the watch for threats from outside. The various departments in a company are often highly dependent on each other but there is at the same time always some element of competition, usually for tasks or resources. Most units tend to formulate goals that will make them encroach on ground regarded by other units as theirs. There is also competition for status and economic rewards – always in short supply in organizations.

We now come to the leadership function that holds the central position in classical theory, namely the job of guiding the unit towards given goals. Traditionally this general function has been further divided into planning, coordinating and control – a division that may perhaps have a certain pedagogical value but is also open to criticism. One objection has been that it is difficult to distinguish clearly between planning and control on the one hand and coordination on the other since coordination is achieved by means of the other two.

The above comments indicate that the tasks a leader may be called upon to fulfil are many and varied. Equally varied are the circumstances in which leaders may have to act. As a result of this, sometimes one leader-

ship function and sometimes another may be the most important, depending on the requirements of the particular situation.
Unfortunately even modern research has little to say about these different types of circumstance and, consequently, about the different demands that are made on leadership. For instance we are still woefully ignorant of the demands likely in periods of decline and those likely in periods of expansion; or, to take quite a different example, of the demands that are most important in the process or the mass production industries.
As regards possible differences in leadership at various levels in the hierarchy, Fayol made certain points sixty years ago which have since been faithfully repeated in most text-books. The most important of these was the proposition that leadership at lower levels requires more technical but less administrative knowledge.

LEADERSHIP METHODS

If we are to develop the thesis that behavior in organizations can be influenced in many different ways – that there is no one method by which people can be led – we shall need a more adequate model of the organization and the individual organization member. The main contribution of modern organization theory has been to replace the classical model of the individual controlled by orders from above by a model of a person who solves problems and makes decisions.
This modified view has come about partly as a result of the changing conditions in organizations described above. It seems that leaders use two main methods in trying to come to terms with the situation. Either they try to maintain various informal sanctions as a source of authority or, and this is probably the more usual, they seek new methods of influencing their subordinates to replace the traditional giving of orders. Some of these methods will be discussed below.
According to the modern view, the behavior of the organization member is based on more or less conscious decisions. These are reached in much the same way as has been described above in our discussion of general decision-making. The decisions of the individual will thus be affected by his goals and by his conception of the present situation. His goals are admittedly complex and changeable and his view of the situation often extremely subjective, but within these limits it is assumed that his be-

havior will nevertheless be fairly systematic. He is also reasonably capable of dealing even with complicated situations and can to some extent adjust to new circumstances.

A person's decisions can consequently be influenced in three ways: by influencing his goals, by influencing his conception of the situation or by changing his ability to solve problems, in particular his ability to discover new action alternatives (cf Fig. 26). In other words there will always be a number of methods by which a manager can influence his subordinates. Here are a few examples.

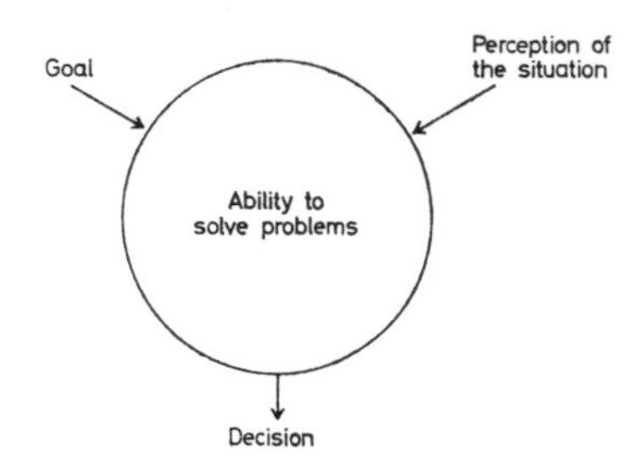

Figure 26. Diagram illustrating the organization member with his ability to solve problems and make decisions. According to organization theory it is more fruitful to regard the member as having these abilities than to see him as merely receiving orders.

How can the goals of an organization member be influenced? He can either be encouraged to accept certain prescribed goals or to identify himself with the organization, the work group or the "general public interest" to the extent that he comes to accept the group goal as his own. How can his ability to solve problems be developed? He can be trained and given the opportunity to broaden his experience. How can his conception of situations be affected? Again by training or by providing him with more information. And finally a method of influencing him which is often very effective is to change the technical environment in which he operates.

LEADERS ARE MANY

The principle of the unity of leadership is one of the pivots of traditional organization theory. Admittedly the line-staff theory implies some modification of the principle, but on the whole it can be claimed that practically no other proposition is as firmly supported in most organizations, at any rate officially, as the one that "each person shall have only one boss". The statement that persons or groups in organizations are actually controlled by impulses from many different sources may therefore strike many as almost blasphemous. However, empirical studies have confirmed it over and over again.

In so far as we accept the picture of the organization member who can solve problems and make decisions as a realistic model, we must also accept that anyone who can be regarded as a reliable source of information is able to wield influence. And although we may agree with the classical argument that behavior is controlled in the main by authoritative messages, we find that modern theory recognizes the many guises of authority. The authority officially delegated to the formal leader through his placing in the organizational chart only reflects in part his influence (cf chapter 4).

The new theory also decrees that decisions in organizations are not usually the work of one person; the decision-making process is divided among many. One person identifies the problem calling for a decision, others supply goals and norms, various people suggest possible alternative courses of action and perhaps a committee tries to determine and evaluate the consequences of the various alternatives.

Nor, generally, is the final choice of alternative – the formal decision – made by any one individual. For various reasons joint decision-making in one form or another takes place at this stage too, so that a decision is made only when two or more persons agree on which decision is the right one. The proposition of classical organization theory that at any rate in situations of conflict the decision is referred to a superior, frequendy turns out in fact to be quite impracticable. Apart from anything else, top managers would just not be able to cope with the burden, and in any case they are often not familiar enough with the problems concerned either to be able or to be willing to resolve conflicts.

But most important of all is the custom employed in most large organizations of deciding things by the application of general policies or decisions. This is particularly marked in the case of personnel problems where, even in relatively small companies, there are often carefully regulated instructions covering most contingencies. In fact the trend towards impersonal decision-making has gone so far in recent years as a result of developments in the technique of data processing, that many observers feel justified in speaking of mechanical or automated decision-making. Thus in many large companies today it is possible to find examples of important decisions about purchasing (e.g. quantities) or sales (e.g. delivery times) which are not made by people at all but by machines. Naturally the operating instructions or decision program was originally worked out by a human brain, but the brain was probably that a of specialist, maybe a consultant from outside the company.

We have seen that the classical view of decision-making makes it easy to underestimate the influence of the stakeholders on the goals and policy of a company; equally it can give rise to an exaggerated view of the actual amount of influence that superiors have over their subordinates. The classical tenet that "the organization shall be plain and clear" has probably helped to prevent decision-making being more split up than it has been. Perhaps there is some advantage in this but a certain disadvantage is that the initiative of the individual organization member has been unnecessarily repressed. It is therefore hardly surprising that while "clear organization" (with a clearly defined formal role system) seems, according to empirical studies, to favour success in more static conditions, it is less likely to do so in a very dynamic environment.

Despite all efforts to stabilize and simplify inter-role relationships, it is nevertheless quite common for these to change character from one moment to the next. Take authority for instance: we may quite likely find that while A wields authority over B in certain circumstances, the roles are reversed a few minutes later when a new situation arises. Also a leader can both add to or consume his "stock" of authority. And, lastly, the various functions of leadership may well be handled by different persons. Quite a common division of roles is as follows: the formal leader formulates goals and handles contacts with the environment, one of his aims being to defend the organizational unit against threats; someone else, an assistant or deputy manager, is responsible for planning and controlling current operations; and a third leader may fulfil an important function in holding the unit together – perhaps he is the most popular member or the "information center".

THE MISUNDERSTOOD ROLE OF BOSS

The picture that we have presented here of the functions and methods of leadership is not intended in any way to diminish the importance of the individual leader. Experienced business leaders have objected with great vehemence that the modern theory – in particular the suggestion that the individual is controlled by impulses from many different sources – implies "a serious undermining of the important boss-subordinate relationship". In several respects this reveals a misunderstanding of the theory.

In fact there is no intention of taking a stand on the old and emotionally loaded question of whether one person can or ought to have more than one boss. To begin with, the new theory is not normative; it is simply intended to describe conditions as they are. Secondly it is quite possible to combine a normative rule that every subordinate shall have only one boss with an acceptance of the fact that he is also controlled by impulses from all round him. The important thing is to know what the normative rule means – that is, what is meant by being a boss.

A serious weakness of classical theory is its doctrinaire refusal to admit the inevitable limits of the powers of the individual leader. In a modern company the boss does not even formally have unlimited power over his subordinates. On a number of questions he can at best pass on decisions and orders stemming from his own superiors or act as the channel of information from others. Frequently he is bound by company policy and other rules fixed by management or accepted by custom. He is also tied by agreements between management and the employees. And, too, he is dependent on a number of specialists, some of whom may be his own subordinates. His authority is limited and, on account of inability or lack of interest, he has abandoned many of the important functions of leadership to others.

In any discussion of industrial democracy it is very important that the role of the boss is understood in this more realistic way. Only thus can the debate be freed from misleading simplifications, with one camp crying "don't tie the hands of the bosses" and the other "down with the arbitrary powers of the boss'."

In so far as the company's goals are accepted by its members, management and the employees will obviously have the same interests, namely that all decisions in the company be as rational as possible, avoiding the subjective or arbitrary; that situations and goals, rather than individuals determine decisions; that the boss functions as the interpreter of the needs of the situation. To a great extent this last interest is in fact the role that organization planners try to assign to managers at different levels.

Many precautions are taken against the individual exercise of arbitrary powers. Examples are: formalizing and indoctrinating the goals of the company, codifying a company policy, indicating rules and supplying instructions for certain types of decision and prescribing joint decision-making or consultation with specialists. And even where the boss has the right of decision, the meaning of this is often much misunderstood. The right of decision does not empower its holder to make any decision he likes; rather it obliges him to make a rational evaluation, after taking into account the company's goals, norms and plans and the needs of the situation at the time.

It would be a mistake to conclude from all this that there is no longer any need for a formal leader or boss. The help of skilled and experienced leaders is still without comparison the most usual and in many cases certainly the best way of discharging most of the necessary functions of leadership. Despite its many weaknesses the hierarchical system has two characteristics in particular which make it clearly superior to all other methods of leadership: its simplicity and its roots in tradition. It might be interesting to quote here an author who made very extensive studies of the problem of leadership and sharply critized the authoritarian style. When he subsequently himself had the opportunity of experiencing the position of the leader as head of a large organization, he reported as follows:

> "Before coming to Antioch, I had observed and worked with top executives as an adviser in a number of top organizations. I thought I knew how they felt about their responsibilities and what led them to behave as they did. I even thought that I could create a role for myself which would enable me to avoid some of the difficulties they encountered.
>
> I was wrong. It took the direct experience of becoming a line executive and meeting personally the problems involved to teach me what no amount of observation of the people could have taught.
>
> I believed, for example, that a leader could operate successfully as a kind of adviser to his organization. I thought I could avoid being a "boss". Unconsciously, I suspect, I hoped to duck the unpleasant necessity of making difficult decisions, of taking the responsibility for one course of action among many uncertain alternatives, of making mistakes and taking the consequences. I thought that maybe I could operate so that everyone would like me – that "good human relations" would eliminate all discord and disagreement.
>
> I couldn't have been more wrong. It took a couple of years, but I finally began to realize that a leader cannot avoid the exercise of authority any more than he can avoid responsibility for what happens to his organization". (McGregor, 1954, p. 261)

CONCLUSIONS

We have already mentioned in an earlier chapter that scientific attempts to draw up simple formulae for successful leadership have not yet led to any conclusive result. In the present chapter we have indicated some at least of the main reasons for this failure. To put it briefly, leadership is much more complicated and variegated than had been assumed in earlier studies. We have emphasized here in particular that leadership has other functions than to guide a unit towards prescribed goals; also in any one group the methods of leadership – and, indeed, the leaders – are many.

Our picture of the complicated nature of leadership in organizations should not be regarded solely as a warning to those who would believe in simple, general prescriptions for harmonizing the needs of the individual and the organization. An admission of the complex nature of leadership affects our thinking in another way too: it means that there are probably a very great many guises in which leadership can appear. Empirical studies confirm this. There is good reason to hope that many essentially different, but from the organization's point of view equally satisfactory, ways of devising the system of leadership are available.

In fact the whole system of leadership – and not just the individual leader – should be regarded as an interesting object of study. There is room for much inventiveness and imagination. Unfortunately up to now classical organization theory has proved a drag on progress. It has been so definite in declaring one method of leadership as the "most suitable", that it has inhibited much possibly rewarding experiment.

Technological developments – perhaps automation in particular – seem likely to help in this respect. Maybe effective leadership systems could be designed that are also conducive of good relations between leader and led and of greater job satisfaction. But, a warning: this cannot just happen of its own accord; effort and thought must go into making the most of the new opportunities.

In the next chapter we shall return to this question. We shall also make a more systematic attempt to apply our theoretical framework in an analysis of the problems encountered in the debate on industrial democracy.

CHAPTER 7
THE IDEOLOGY AND PROGRAM OF INDUSTRIAL DEMOCRACY – A FIRST ANALYSIS

INTRODUCTION

Background, Aims and Content

Now the time has come to draw together the strands running through this book and to analyze some of the questions spotlighted in the debate on industrial democracy. A general starting-point for such an analysis was indicated in rough outline in our introductory chapter. It seemed that there were two main causes of the confusion that has hampered worth-while discussions in this area. First the statement of *goals* and the consideration of practical *means* of achieving the goals desired have not always been kept separate. Secondly, those partaking in the debate have lacked a common frame of reference and – more serious still – a theory of the company and its organization, which could have facilitated a systematic analysis of the relations between means and ends.

The task of this book, perhaps rather ambitious and far-seeking, has therefore been to try to sum up and present some part of such a theory. With this purpose in mind, the middle and most comprehensive section of the book, included the posing of such questions as: What is meant by the goals and policy of a company? What factors influence them? How can conflicts between the parties on the labor market be influenced? Is technology an important factor affecting the workers' chances of job satisfaction? Is any one leadership style clearly superior? What is the difference between influence and co-determination? How can the status and authority of, for instance, a works council be increased?

This emphasis on the theoretical accords fully with our repeated declaration that the main purpose of the book is to suggest and develop a common frame of reference for those taking part in the debate. Nonetheless, something must be said in conclusion about how the suggested theory can be applied and some illustrative examples be provided.

Back to the Kernel of the Debate: Ideology and Program

In chapter 1 some examples were given of the type of question that can and ought to be raised. Before embarking on the present discussion we can remind the reader of some of these and add a few others.

First we have to ask: What are the desired goals of industrial democracy? The answer can be sought in the words of the many debaters who can also be asked to clarify their views. Various tests can be made to see whether the goals thus revealed agree with actual objectives. It is not unusual in debates of this type to find that even those involved are not altogether clear about their final goals. Is it not be expected, in a dynamic society like ours, that there will be a gradual but continuous shift in goals? And which groups accept, or identify themselves with, the various objectives? Is there general agreement about goals or is there some conflict between groups? Does the ideology of industrial democracy agree with any other ideology? Are the various subgoals compatible or not?

In any examination of the practical program it is natural to start in the same way by asking: What programs exist? Are the various items practicable? What is expected of them? Is it likely that they will lead to the desired results? Will they also have other consequences? Are these acceptable? Can certain measures be combined in such a way as to mitigate the less desirable consequences? Are there other more efficient ways of achieving any of the goals? Why have some items on the program but not others, earned the rubric "democratic"?

There are many different ways of tackling these questions. It might seem natural to discuss first some of the most important points in the ideological program and for each one analyze possible ways of attaining them. We have chosen another method: to approach the whole network of problems at once, but from three starting-points.

If we accept the approach and terminology presented in chapter 3 (on conflict and cooperation), we can say that the debate on industrial democracy reflects part of a continuous process of conflict resolution, in which the claims and demands of the employees encounter those of the other stakeholders. With this in mind it seems natural to view and study the situation from the points of view of the parties concerned. And this is what we will now do. On a basis of the theory presented in the main section of this book, we will try to show how "industrial democracy" can be understood from the point of view of management and of the trade unions. Lastly, in a concluding section, we will choose a third starting-point for our analysis, from which a suggestion for reformulating the central questions will be evolved.

Under the first two headings we will discuss questions of the type exemplified above, but without trying to impose any strict system. When used in analysis, the theory formulated here proves much more fruitful on some questions that on others; we will therefore limit ourselves to those questions for which there is some foundation, although this means that our discussion cannot claim to be complete.

MANAGEMENT AND INDUSTRIAL DEMOCRACY

When examining "industrial democracy" from the point of view of management we assume that management is likely to view the goals and the practical program suggested in the light of the goals and methods pertaining to its own role as business leader. We will therefore precede our analysis with a recapitulation – on some points an elaboration – of our earlier picture of the principles and techniques of management.

Background: Goals and Methods of Management

The primary goal of managerial activities is the survival and, if possible. the development and expansion of the company. This does not mean – the point is worth repeating – that managers are all idealists. The goal, thus defined, also enables management to satisfy its own economic and egoistic needs.

From this follow, among other things, two subgoals: to see that operations are efficient and rational and to try to assure good relations between the company and its stakeholders, i.e. the owners, customers, suppliers, employees etc. The claims made by the stakeholders on the company must, to some extent at any rate, be satisfied. Seldom or never can they be wholly so. Thus management often sees itself as defender of the organization against threats implied by the claims of the stakeholders – not only of the employees but of the owners and the others too. It is not just empty words when a well-known Swedish business leader declares: "But an industry can be throttled by demanding too much profit today without having regard for the morrow – just as it can be throttled by demanding too much tomorrow. The main goal must be to survive." (Quoted in the Swedish daily newspaper, Dagens Nyheter, 1962).

In a previous section, in which we discussed company goals, it was pointed out that there exists a whole hierarchy of goals and that daily operations are not usually guided by the superior ones, but rather by a number of subsidiary goals, plans and norms. To realize these goals, management has some highly developed techniques at its disposal. In view of the ever-growing complexity of these aids, top management has become increasingly dependent on support from specialists. The methods and tools available have been classified in many different ways. For our present purpose it is natural to see them grouped around the two subgoals mentioned above. One group of methods is then mainly concerned with controlling and increasing the efficiency of the organization and another with "handling" the stakeholders, or seeing to the maintenance of good relations.

The first group of methods includes amongst other things planning, budgeting and control systems, work and methods studies, office efficiency techniques etc. To the second group belong, for example, advertising, PR and personnel administration. Some management techniques are more difficult to categorize, for instance product design and development (both of which can streamline production but also increase the product's attraction for the customer), piece work and bonus systems (which can lead to a more effective use of working time and to a higher degree of job satisfaction) and auditing (which can favorably affect internal efficiency and can also act as a guarantee vis-à-vis owners and creditors).

If we are to discuss management's conception of industrial democracy, it is very important to emphasize the advanced stage of development of these managerial aids and their continual exposure to further change. The average company has thus often had time to adopt only some of the aids. And, to some extent, this selectiveness can be justified: many of the methods are both costly and liable to produce various undesirable side effects. The relatively sparse use of this arsenal of aids can also be explained by the lack of competent personnel, management's native caution and the functioning of our old friend "management-by-exception". As long as things are "working OK", many a business leader will take little interest in possibly risky changes in his organization or administrative system.

Management Regards Some Aspects of Industrial Democracy as Constructive

As is well known, many business leaders have shown a positive interest in certain forms of industrial democracy. In many countries, managers have even been pioneers in promoting various "democratic" measures, voluntarily and without pressure from their employees. However, it is interesting to note the variety of argument that has been invoked in support of their actions. We find on examination that arguments fall into two main classes, relating to what has just been said about the goals and methods of management.

1. The business leader feels that certain of his own goals coincide with what he understands to be the goals of industrial democracy.
2. He feels that parts of the program of industrial democracy will advance the achievement of his own goals.

If this line of reasoning is pursued further, we can perhaps assume that management sees all efforts towards industrial democracy as, first and foremost, an aid in achieving higher productivity and greater efficiency. Managers are therefore prepared to support suggestions, schemes or consultation about productivity, safety precautions, machine maintenance and quality control.

But our theory suggests that such measures will not be particularly successful. Industrial engineering is a task for specialists and the majority of employees cannot be expected to feel greatly encouraged or inspired by the fact that, for instance, a few chosen representatives are offered the chance of sitting on consultative committees.

Moreover managers cannot help questioning whether certain of the measures will help or hinder in their "handling" of the stakeholders Will a new channel of information, for instance, strengthen their position in negotiation? Managers who have experience of acute conflicts with the employees are perhaps prepared to try some of the suggested methods, hoping to avoid wasteful and costly developments. Others hope that such measures will improve their contact with the employees, thus increasing the chances for employee identification with the company. Yet others, worried by the strength of a trade union, may weigh the possibilities of being able to play off the works council against the union. Others ask: can "industrial democracy" help to make the company's position more secure?

At the same time, though, management is suspicious: the balance of power is sensitive and the mechanism of conflict resolution easily disturbed; there is a risk in initiating measures whose consequences are not easy to foresee.

But can we not expect that at least a few individual business leaders may see something constructive in some of the democratic measures, for other and perhaps more idealistic reasons than those mentioned above? According to existing theory the answer is probably "yes", although there will naturally be considerable individual variation. What does seem clear, however, is that many leaders, at any rate in certain situations, really go a long way towards identifying themselves with their employees and do regard as their own goal the best interest of the employees, as they see it.

Management Regards Some Aspects of Industrial Democracy with Doubt and Misgiving

We have discussed the large group of business leaders among whom there is a positive attitude towards what is usually known as "industrial democracy". But there are many others who air decidedly critical and sometimes even directly negative views. Rather than condemn these managers without further ado as conservative and greedy for power and profit, why not examine what explanations of their objections and doubts scientific theory can provide. We can use the same division as above and pose the following questions:

1. Could some of the ideas embodied in the movement towards industrial democracy be regarded by business leaders as incompatible with their own goals and norms?

2. Among the practical suggestions are there any whose consequences the business leader could not regard as desirable and which would therefore naturally arouse his misgivings?

The most serious objection probably concerns demands for greater employee influence and less managerial freedom of action. It has been pointed out earlier that the business leader finds it typical of his situation that his freedom of action is often so circumscribed. This is particularly marked in times of recession. To ease this situation he strives to create good relations with the stakeholders and lay up reserves for the future, thus assuring the company of the security proffered by a certain amount of freedom of action. What others regard as the manager's "freedom", for example to increase or decrease production, introduce new products or transfer operations, is felt by the manager himself as the force of circumstances. He does not possess unlimited freedom to introduce such changes whenever he feels like it – such changes represent the manager's attempt to meet up to the demands placed on him by his situation.

Another point in the discussion of industrial democracy which might be expected to irritate many business leaders is the way in which the demand for efficiency and high productivity is neglected in favor of other goals. It is very important to remember here that, whether we call it materialism or idealism, the satisfaction and self respect of the business leader depend to a very high degree on his self-image as responsible for one of the most important functions of the community: the production of goods and services. He wants others, too, to acknowledge the importance of his contribution.

From the manager's point of view, these represent very serious objections to any program of industrial democracy which seeks either to increase employee influence at the expense of management's freedom of action, or to increase job-satisfaction regardless of the demand for high productivity.

Proceeding from the theory presented above, we can expect the business leader to raise objections of another kind against most of the practical measures that are generally suggested. We mentioned earlier that the principle of "management-by-exception" creates what we have called management's natural inaction. The principle can also be regarded as a kind of defensive mechanism, enabling management to concentrate on the most important tasks. After all, in any company there is an almost unlimited field for possible improvements. Nor is there usually any lack of ideas and suggestions.

On the other hand the resources for studying and analyzing the suggestions, let alone for putting them into practice, are very limited. In particular there is great pressure on managements' time, interest and energy. Mainly for this reason many of the modern administrative aids are not fully utilized in the majority of companies. Add to this managements' general tendency to caution when faced with the new and the untried, and it is not surprising and quite understandable to find the reaction: "But we have so much else to do that is more important".

As a result of continuing specialization and improvements in technical aids, operations in large modern companies are nowadays led and controlled by various methods other than the simple giving of commands from boss to subordinate. It is important to take this change into account in any analysis of organizational conditions, but it would be wrong to presume without further ado that the development brings nothing but benefit. On the contrary, the undermining of "the line" is regarded in many companies as a serious problem. This is further aggravated by the necessity to coordinate the many specialists and avoid conflict between them (the staff) and the ordinary line managers. It is therefore natural for a business leader to wonder anxiously whether some of the practical forms for increasing employee influence may make the situation even worse. The direct contact between employees and management could easily result in removing the lower managers even further from the actual managing of operations. And might not the works council – and in particular perhaps its special sub-committees responsible for suggestions, machine maintenance, quality control, safety etc – increase the risk of conflict, in this case with the various specialist bodies responsible for matters in the same spheres?

THE TRADE UNIONS AND INDUSTRIAL DEMOCRACY

A similar analysis of the attitude of the trade unions to the principles and practices of industrial democracy shows some interesting parallels. It is perhaps worth pointing out that the following is *not* based on statements made by trade unionists. Our only purpose is to predict, on the basis of the theory presented above, something of what leading trade unionists would be likely to think about industrial democracy and what they could hope to achieve by it.

Background: Goals and Methods of the Trade Unions

In the theoretical part of this book one chapter was devoted to a theory of organizational goals. A trade union is an organization, so let us briefly apply this theory to its goals.

With our way of looking at things, a trade union, like an industrial company, can be regarded as having both a management as well as stakeholders. The most important stakeholders are the individual member groups, another group includes the companies employing members. Such a suggestion may at first seem almost shocking. But it would be unrealistic not to accept that the unions are dependent on cooperation with the companies, just as the companies are dependent on cooperation with the unions. It can thus also be expected that the union leader will often have to act as mediator both among member groups and between these groups and the companies.

The leader of a trade union can be expected, like his colleagues the company managers, to identify himself with his organization. Its survival and improvement is for him essential and can only be achieved if he formulates goals and runs operations in such a way that all the stakeholders regard the organization as worthy of their support. As the company must provide the customers with goods, the employee with wages, the owner with dividends, etc, so must a trade union with any hope of a stable and progressive future, provide essential services; it must for example look after the economic interests of its members and guarantee industrial peace. A company feeling hard competition makes strenuous efforts through marketing, advertising, product development etc to increase the size of a particular group of stakeholders, namely customers. "Hard competition" is in some ways similar to the situation of most unions. The trade union is forced to make strenuous efforts through marketing, and often through achieving concrete material benefits for its members in order to attract and maintain members (customers).

Most people's idea of the business leader is that he does not consider the stakeholders as completely equal, but identifies himself more with the owners than with the others. Similarly the general view of the trade union leader is probably that he usually identifies himself with the union members rather than with the other stakeholders, for example the community or the company. It would be interesting to test this empirically; it would not be surprising if the idea proved to be considerably exaggerated.

The trade unions have developed advanced techniques and collected considerable resources with which to work for their goals. The picture is well known and need only be summarized very briefly here. The branch of their operations which at one time dominated entirely and is still the most important for Scandinavian trade unions, is negotiation with employers and with the employer organizations. In this sphere they now recognize a growing need for statistical and economic research to provide a sound basis for negotiations. However, their operations have gradually been supplemented by an increasing number of activities aimed at stimulating members to greater engagement in the union. The education of members, particularly of those active in the movement, has been geared to improving efficiency in the organization and to binding the members to the movement. In recent years the activities of the works' councils have been added.

The trade unions also need to renew their program and methods continuously in order to be able to satisfy new claims from the stakeholders. Moreover, in a changing environment, old methods tend to become ineffective, even if objectives are still the same.

The Trade Unions Regard Some Aspects of Industrial Democracy as Constructive

There is good foundation for expecting the trade unions to take a very positive attitude towards most of the principles and practices that go under the name of industrial democracy.

As in the case of management there are probably two main explanations:

1. It seems that certain trade union goals coincide with what are understood to be the goals of industrial democracy.
2. It seems that some of the practical suggestions will help in the achievement of union goals.

Under the first of these headings we find all efforts to increase employee influence, thereby providing employees with opportunities for upholding their interests in the company in competition with the other stakeholders. This, as we know, is also one of the main goals of the trade union movement.

The trade unions can also be expected to support any measures which will help the employees to find satisfaction other than the purely economic in their work. As with many other organizations, the trade unions continually run the risk of reducing their own inner strength because their very achievements render their services less necessary. Therefore, if they wish to retain their old clientèle, they must always have an eye to new needs to satisfy, and perhaps even themselves to create such needs. There is a surprisingly close parallel here with many of the marketing problems of the consumer goods industries.

Loyalty to the company combined with an understanding of the general benefits of higher productivity should arouse union support for measures intended to increase productivity. The greatest enthusiasm will presumably be for improvements that directly benefit the employees, for example suggestion schemes and consultation on safety measures.

If we turn to practical suggestions, the trade unions could be expected to most readily support any measures that contribute directly to the status and prestige of the movement. Thus anything that extended the scope and influence of the works councils, thereby making them a really important factor, acknowledged as such by both management and employees, and perhaps even representation on the board, would be regarded as attractive possibilities.

The Trade Unions Regard Some Aspects of Industrial Democracy with Doubt and Misgiving

The fact that the trade union movement is positive in its attitude towards most of the principles and practices of industrial democracy does not mean that we cannot expect a negative reaction to at least some aspects, in particular to some of the practical suggestions. Every proposal that involves the establishment of institutions alongside the trade unions, with the accompanying risk to the latter of losing in real importance, status and prestige, must be regarded by them as a serious threat. Competition for the interest and support of the employees in any typical "union" sphere cannot be easily tolerated.

A works council with the right of decision, employee representation on the board and profit-sharing systems could all, at least in some cases, be regarded as competitors of the trade unions in their role as defender of employee interests. Perhaps this doubt is well founded, if, as has been claimed, some of the management pioneers of work councils saw in these institutions an effective way of keeping the unions out of internal problems.

Bearing in mind the theory presented in chapters 3 and 4, however, it also seems likely that several of the practical measures, if likely to upset the balance of power in the company, will be received by the trade unions with reservations. Take, for example, a change in the established technique for resolving conflict: it is rather difficult to tell in advance whether it will increase or diminish the unions' chances of upholding their legitimate interests. Nor is it by any means certain that the granting of the formal right of decision on certain questions will actually increase the power and influence of the employees in the works council.

The same applies to employee representation on management or the board. In an earlier section this was described as an example of coöptation, one of the most effective ways of defending an organization against an aggressive and influential stakeholder. Experienced trade union leaders will obviously be fully aware of the delicate and unpredictable nature of such a situation. Moreover we observed that a group or organization involved in conflict, particularly in acute conflict, strengthens its internal loyalty. The trade unions are therefore likely to view any such commitments to management with grave doubt. Would they not lose, in the eye of their members, their all-important standing as defender of employee interests?

KEY QUESTIONS IN THE DEBATE ON INDUSTRIAL DEMOCRACY A SUGGESTED REFORMULATION

We have now examined the ideology and practical program of industrial democracy from two quite different points of view. We have tried to appreciate how management and the trade unions each look upon these matters and how they feel about the current debate.

Perhaps the most interesting result of this analysis is a definite motivation to a suspicion at which we hinted in our very first chapter: The frames of reference of the business manager and the trade union leader are so basically dissimilar that although they may both speak of "industrial democracy", they are referring in many essential respects to different things. As regards ends or means, principles or practices, the confusion is the same. Thus, if we succeeded in defining the various suggestions and evaluations more clearly, it is not unlikely that the differences of opinion would probably only appear the greater.

It can be helpful simply to understand and accept that there are real contradictions here. Otherwise unnecessary factual or formal conflicts may arise making it even more difficult to resolve the conflicts of interest. The many discussions about works councils are a revealing example. It is certainly difficult for managers to understand the arguments of the trade unions on this point, unless they can accept that one of the essential goals of the movement is to find new spheres of activity and to inspire union members to participate. On the other hand the unions may easily misinterpret the lack of interest and enthusiasm of many managers unless they can put themselves in management's shoes, and really feel with management that "so many things are more important".

It is of course impossible for the researcher to say which side is right. They both are, in that both views are logical, given the different backgrounds and goals. However, if we compare the two pictures of "industrial democracy" in the light of the theory developed in our earlier chapters, something else strikes us very strongly, namely that it should be quite possible to reformulate many of the problems to the advantage of clarity and precision. We think it worthwhile here to attempt such a reformulation.

Two Main Questions

In all wide-ranging discussions it is natural to try to pin down and classify the problems. Thus, at the beginning of this book, we claimed that the debate on industrial democracy can be divided into ideological and practical problems.

In the course of general debate, however, other classifications have been suggested. Practical solutions have sometimes been divided into those aiming at influence and those aiming at participation. It has also been quite common to divide the ideological arguments according to whether the main interest lies in the workers as people or in the results of the work done.

This last classification, in particular, has become common. This is not at all surprising. It is simple and convenient, not least because the two lines of argument lend themselves readily to identification with the "main" parties in the debate, i.e. the employees and the employers.

But perhaps, in view of the theory presented in these pages, we can now suggest another meaningful classification. In doing so, we are persuaded that a division based on concrete practical measures is less valuable than one based on objectives. Ends, not means, should govern analysis and discussion. We shall try to show that in fact the whole debate can be geared substantially to two main objectives which can be tentatively formulated thus:

1. To establish a satisfactory balance between the various interests in the company.
2. To establish such working and management methods that the company's operations will lead to the desired result in the most efficient way.

FIRST MAIN QUESTION: BALANCE OF INTERESTS AND THE RESOLUTION OF CONFLICT

One group of questions, of immediate urgency and interest, is concerned with employee power and influence versus managerial freedom of action. Discussions about the possible forms of influence and about industrial conflict also belong to this group. Our view is that these questions are closely related, and since the connecting link is provided by the theory presented in chapters 2-4, a summary of that theory might be in place here.

There is an inevitable contradiction between the claims of the various stakeholders – sometimes even between the claims of one and the same stakeholder. It is nevertheless essential to the functioning of the company that the conflicts are resolved and cooperation and coordination established. Certain methods for resolving conflicts are available. The commodity market, the capital market and the labor market can be regarded as institutions with this function. The existing system of employer-employee negotiation and consultation, and the machinery for settling disputes, both work towards the same end.

An essential objective for every relevant social program – whether it be called "industrial democracy" or something else – must be *to try to contribute to the development of the best possible methods and institutions for resolving conflicts and establishing cooperation.*

What, then, is required of the methods and institutions for resolving conflicts between stakeholders? There appear to be two main types of demand. First, it seems to be a basic democratic principle to seek some sort of balance between various interests. Secondly, it seems to be required that the institutions should not be too costly, i.e. should be as free as possible from undesirable side effects.

We have not the space here to consider the meaning of these demands more closely. A few comments, mainly to indicate the complexity of the questions, must suffice. Furthermore, we will restrict ourselves to the methods for resolving a clash of interests between employees and other stakeholders in the company (represented by management).

If we look first at the "costs", two circumstances in particular seem to arouse general misgivings. Surely, runs the argument, there must be ways of avoiding acute conflicts, with all the inconvenience that they cause and the aggressions that they nourish.

Further, do not present methods for resolving conflicts needlessly exclude the employees from problem-solving and decision-making? And doesn't this create problems when it comes to realizing plans and attaining the goals prescribed? We will now consider how far this criticism is justified.

Are Present Methods for Resolving Conflicts Unnecessarily Costly?

A serious disadvantage of present forms of employee influence is the "negative" character: employees can make their claims and exclude certain alternative courses of action. This could be labelled uneconomical, and not only because it prevents employees from contributing to general discussion and to the search for better alternatives. There are other uneconomic aspects too.

A main purpose of prescribing clear goals, norms and plans, is to provide good grounds for loyal cooperation and effective coordination. Some business leaders with experience of powerful works councils or consultative committees, have reported a falling-off in unreasonable claims from employees. If people feel that the demands they do make are given proper attention, they will probably be prepared to drop those that are more extreme. There is probably too some real guarantee of their loyal cooperation in working for the goals prescribed.

It is felt by many that the official channels do not provide a suitable line of communication in this case. A number of scientific studies are quoted in support. Employees are not keen to make their wishes known that way; any claims that do reach the lower managers generally get no further. Thus, unless special steps are taken, management is likely to formulate unrealistic goals, norms and plans which the employees cannot accept. This can well result in acute conflict. Even where better procedures for consultation do exist, acute conflicts cannot be entirely avoided, but they can be discovered in time and resolved before becoming a serious obstacle to cooperation.

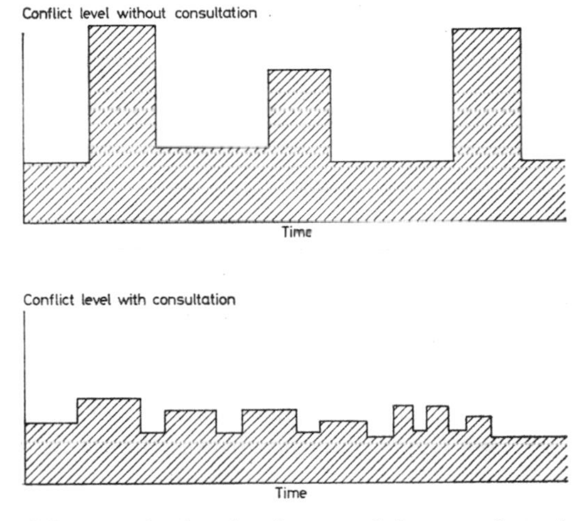

Figure 27. The Glacier Metal Company has introduced an extended system of consultative committees. The Managing Director of the Company claims that it is consequently easier to discover conflicts between management and the employees at an earlier and less serious stage.

One might easily be tempted to object that the normal channels between boss and subordinate and between management and union *ought* to provide adequate opportunity for the free flow of information. This objection has in fact often been made by those who do not see any need for special consultative bodies. Despite quite extensive research, it is difficult to decide who is right. In the next chapter we shall return to the question of whether it is even likely that one side is right and the other wrong.

There is, however, another catch in the argument that unreservedly favors new procedures for consultation. And that is the categoric assumption that acute conflicts are always a bad thing. That conflict with other groups is an active means of increasing loyalty within an organization has been emphasized on several occasions and frequently confirmed. We can therefore go further and say that, if strong trade unions are considered desirable, conflicts between employer and employees must be regarded as having at least some desirable effects. In any case, it can hardly be in the interests of the trade unions to support measures that link the unions to management and involve them in the responsibility for the survival and success of the company.

Thus we cannot simply condemn present methods for resolving conflicts as ineffective and unnecessarily costly. Naturally, they could be improved, but the pros and cons of both present methods and possible improvements should be carefully examined.

Have Employees Enough Influence?

Before trying to answer the question headlined here, we might perhaps remind the reader of a point already mentioned in chapter 2. We said there that an unspecified demand for employee influence in the company is misleading since it implies a total lack of such influence at the present time. We suggested further that the general claim for "influence" might be based on a misunderstanding of the true conditions. How likely is this?

In the case of experienced trade union officials, it is hardly possible to dismiss the demand for employee influence as the result of a misunderstanding. In Sweden a competent observer once said that a certain impatience with all the talk about capitalist power could sometimes be discerned in the labor camp. "A single trade union leader ... has greater influence than a handful of capitalists". (Wigforss, 1956, p. 51).

There is possibly, however, a general tendency to underestimate the opportunities already available to employees and unions for looking after their interests. This may well be combined with a failure to understand just how many demands converge on company management.

Disregarding such possible misunderstandings, we have tried to show in this chapter that greater influence is a natural goal for the trade unions, regardless of how much influence they already have. And in fact this agrees with the declarations of trade union leaders: "... It is in the nature of a trade union to desire power in the sense of influence and the possibility of bringing pressure to bear. Over the years we have learned that without influence we cannot fulfil our declared duty to defend the interests of the employees. It lies in the whole nature of a trade union to desire and demand influence, but about the boundaries of this influence, we know very little".[1] (Ramsten, 1963) (Our translation).

The demand from employees for greater influence, however, clashes with management's demand for undiminished freedom of action and with the interests of other parties. Let us stand outside the battle and ask: Is it difficult, in the present situation, for employees to uphold their interests vis-à-vis management and the other stakeholders of the company, i.e. the owners, customers, suppliers and society?

This is obviously an extremely difficult and complex question. If we accept that inaction is the natural state of management and action is a pattern of behavior forced upon it, we are faced by the hypothesis that difficult situations and complex demands are a necessary spur. This has been empirically confirmed. Obvious examples are provided by some of the noted public enquiries which have been made on various occasions in both private and public companies, but the hypothesis has been confirmed also in other more systematic studies. High taxation, hard competition, strong trade unions and full employment may perhaps have other negative consequences, but they do at least have the advantage of forcing management to brace itself.

At the same time we must not forget that the demands may grow too big; also that management's goal – the company's survival and expansion – generally represents a long-term objective worthwhile to all parties. Thus management often acts as the balancing force between long-term and short-term interests. Recent discussions about combating inflation have

[1] The definition of power used in this book appears on p. 67.

also shown that it is by no means always socially benefical for management to give way to the short-term demands of the employees.
Finally it may be worth pointing out that management seems likely to have the best chance of satisfying the stakeholders' most urgent demands when these are formulated in very general terms. Take the customer who gives detailed specifications instead of simply demanding certain general standard; or the owner who not only demands a certain return on his capital input but also expects to regulate operations; or the trade unions who not only demand good working conditions but also try to control the organization of the work. All these may perhaps improve their own positions but they also expose management to great difficulty when it comes to satisfying the requirements of the other stakeholders. A prerequisite of a "healthy" balance of interests is that every stakeholder is in a strong position and has a good chance of satisfying his most important needs. At the same time no one stakeholder can promote his own interests disproportionately or impose such detailed regulations that management is unable to satisfy the others.
Thus, although the unions' demand for greater influence clashes with management's desire to cling to its freedom of action, it can be expected that neither party will unreservedly welcome the introduction of measures likely to affect the delicate balance of interests. We refer here again to our earlier contention that it is rather difficult to foresee how any particular change or innovation will affect either party's chances of defending its interests.

Conclusions

In view of all that has been said above, it can be claimed that many Western countries enjoy a considerable measure of industrial democracy. Admittedly any form of leadership that involves the control of one person by another could perhaps be called undemocratic and in this sense the same countries cannot even lay claim to political democracy. The main achievement of political democracy has been to balance the interests and demands of the different social groups. Similar advantages have been gained by other methods in industrial life. There, too, will be found systematic efforts to weigh the claims of different interest groups against each other. Already as things are today, the employees have considerable opportunities of upholding their interests. Naturally this does not mean that democracy in industrial life could not be extended or its methods improved. If a meaningful discussion of this question is to be possible, however, the various arguments and the analysis of the situation need to be filled out in greater detail.

We cannot conclude that further development must include a general increase in employee influence. It may be that we must differentiate between groups of employees and perhaps devote special attention to particular "minority interests" which have greater need for influence. The variations between companies and perhaps even between industries are probably highly significant. Perhaps, too, we must differentiate between the periods of prosperity and recession. It may also be that the employees have adequate opportunities for satisfying some of their demands but lack the means and methods of achieving others. This last point seems to be particularly important, as will be shown below.

SECOND MAIN QUESTION: THE ACHIEVEMENT OF HIGHER PRODUCTIVITY (N.B. BROADER DEFINITION OF PRODUCTIVITY REQUIRED)

Another set of questions that seem closely related are those referring to equality, job satisfaction and new ways of increasing productivity. A connecting link can be provided by the theory presented in chapters 5 and 6. In this connection we would also refer to the interpretation of "productivity" suggested at the end of chapter 6 and based on the theory of the function and goal of the company presented earlier in this book. These propositions can be brought together and summarized as follows.

There is no simple connection between job satisfaction and productivity as traditionally measured (production per input of production factors). Nor is there any simple prescription for designing a production system or choosing the leadership style most likely to realize the goals of maximum job satisfaction or maximum productivity. On the other hand research is beginning to provide us with certain clues. It should be possible, given courageous experiment and detailed study and analysis, to find methods of production and administration more effective in achieving job satisfaction and high productivity than those at present available.

It would be in place here to recapitulate our earlier comments on the concept of productivity. The company is a social and technical system, by means of which it is possible to satisfy certain human and social needs. Which needs will these be? The answer will depend partly on the demands of the various stakeholders and on their relative strength and partly on the production resources and the technology available. For any measure of productivity to be complete, it must include the relation between all the material and psychological needs satisfied by the company and all the material and psychological demands made by the company on its stakeholders.

According to this view the second main goal of industrial democracy will be to encourage higher productivity, understood in this broader sense.

We shall in any case now discuss a program of action, taking this assumed objective as our starting-point.

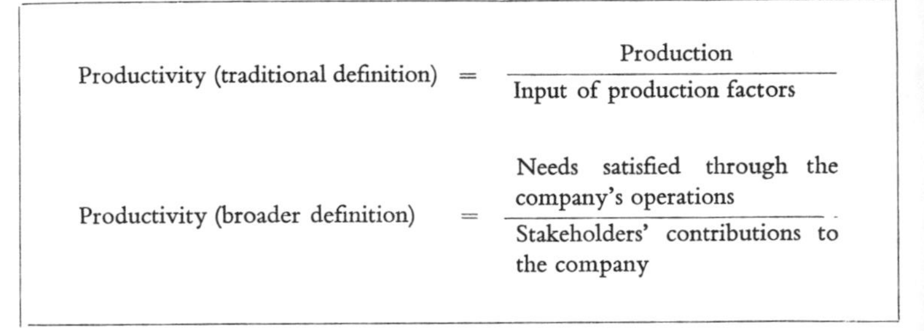

Figure 28. The concept of productivity: a comparison between the traditional and a broader view.

Democracy and Productivity (in the Traditional Sense)

Greater efficiency and productivity is a goal on which management and the employee organizations are often able to agree – nowadays in Scandinavia, almost always. A continuous improvement of productivity is regarded by management as vital to the company. The employees and their organizations have become increasingly aware that their chances of obtaining a better economic return for their labor no longer depend essentially on their strength at the negotiating table. Just as important is that management has something to give, that it can maintain and improve productivity. However, a degree of agreement regarding goals is one thing: we are not so likely to find such accord when it comes to means.

Management and its specialists devote themselves professionally to the task of increasing the efficiency and productivity of the company. As we have already seen, very advanced techniques have been developed. Many of these, however, are inevitably linked to consequences not easily acceptable to the employees. Greater investment in mechanical aids will often lead, in the short run, to a considerable drain on liquid assets and – again in the short run – to less funds for paying wages. Investments of this type and other measures to improve productivity may also create a risk of unemployment in the company concerned or even in a whole professional group or industry. (Management's main counter argument is well known: that a failure to improve productivity lowers the competitive strength of the company and therefore leads to even more certain unemployment in the long run.) Lastly, new production techniques and similar changes may impair working conditions, for instance by requiring greater effort of the employees.

Thus, although the employees and their organizations support in principle measures intended to increase efficiency and productivity, they are also most anxious to be able so to check each measure that it does not threaten their own interests. And they will be inclined to favor those that do not. Suggestion schemes and consultation on working methods, for instance, offer advantages to the employees. They also provide opportunities for constructive influence. But perhaps an ever greater advantage is that they allow the trade unions a say in deciding on matters that directly affect them. To some extent the union can steer the choice away from efficiency measures which are perceived as not lying in their interests.

From management's point of view these advantages are obscured by the obvious risks of overestimating the value and practicability of thus involving the employees in measures of improvements. All measures to increase productivity demand the time and limited resources of management. There are numerous other forces continuously competing for the attention of management. To be successful in this competition, a works council must be unusually productive. This is not hard to understand if one accepts that, for instance, a personnel specialist can probably evaluate the consequences of some measure within his field better than any other employee, however experienced he may be; or that a marketing specialist can judge the value of various marketing strategies better than the most experienced salesman.

New Claims on the Company?

There is one reason in particular why, at the present time, we need a broader concept of productivity. In a prosperous welfare society it can be expected that the stakeholders, in particular the employees, will make new claims on the company over and above their purely "material" demands. The following are some of the questions that therefore come to mind.

What are the new needs that people will expect the company to satisfy? From the point of view of society in general, is it reasonable to try to satisfy these needs at work? Are employees prepared to cut down on other demands in order to satisfy them? Have the employee organizations a clear idea of the needs for which people seek satisfaction? Can management adapt the company's administration and production methods so that the new claims can be satisfied? Can the employees uphold the new claims vis-à-vis the other stakeholders in the company?

Unfortunately we have not been able to give here a consistent account of motivational psychology – the branch of psychology which could best throw some light on this type of question. Our discussion of the problems surrounding job satisfaction, however, has served indirectly to show how little scientific knowledge there is in this sphere. Employees today are thus not very likely to receive much help, at least not from the scientists, in specifying their demands on the company. Moreover the lack of a scientific base increases difficulties in communication, for example between employer and employee, and between the organizations of the two groups.

Despite the difficulties that dog any attempt at clearer definition, it is nevertheless hard to free oneself of the feeling that something is happening. And certainly in all camps – among managers, trade union leaders and politicians – are many who believe that something *should* happen. If we might hazard a guess, it seems likely that the next few years will see the employees and their organizations trying to specify more clearly what they mean by "job satisfaction". It is of course essential to make such a specification before being able to express definite claims and demanding their fulfilment.

Ideally the new claims should be expressed not only qualitatively but, to some extent, also quantitatively. In any case if broader demands are to have hope of satisfaction, the problem of measurement must somehow be solved. But that alone is not enough. The new claims must also be accepted as legitimate. Otherwise it is highly probable that some demands, actually referring to something else, will appear in the guise of another "permitted" claim. The most obvious example could be a continued emphasis on demands for higher money wages and shorter working hours, after these have really ceased to hold such a central position. Or, for lack of an accepted and "legitimate" alternative, the trade union movement might let one or other form of co-determination become a goal in itself.

Industrial Democracy and Productivity (in the Broad Sense)

Assuming that management (either on its own initiative or under pressure from the employees) is willing to extend its goals to include maximum employee job satisfaction, the most effective ways of doing this will not be those usually discussed in connection with industrial democracy. Consultative committees, profit sharing schemes or representation on the board are not likely to make much real difference to the majority of employees. More effective would be consultation between boss and subordinate and, in fact, the general leadership methods of the various managers. A democratic leadership style (participative management) need not necessarily lead to higher productivity in the traditional sense. But if the concept of productivity is extended to include job satisfaction and employee attitudes, the picture will be different. We then find that a leadership style in which every manager systematically consults his subordinates before making many of his decisions will have a beneficial effect on "productivity".

According to some results of recent research it seems that the most effective method, however, involves radical changes in working methods and thereby in the whole working milieu. At the same time it has been pointed out that this is an extremely complicated and all-embracing process and one which is still in its early days. Up to now there is very little practical experience of the possibilities. It cannot be overemphasized in this context, that any program for increasing productivity must be adapted to the demands and possibilities of the individual situation.

Conclusions

A second main goal of industrial democracy could thus be described as higher productivity, defined in a broader sense than the traditional. It is not easy at the present time to say how this can best be achieved. On this point, as on others, it is difficult not to be critical of most of the conventional programs for extending industrial democracy. The goal is important and urgent – but it seems that to achieve it we need to explore new paths.

CHAPTER 8

SOME CONCLUDING REMARKS

STARTING-POINT FOR A NEW DISCUSSION?

In our opening chapter we observed that the rallying cry "industrial democracy" has been persistently heard in a debate – which at least in Scandinavia seems to be of ever-growing dimensions. We also concluded that a study of what has actually been said leaves only a vague impression of what the debate is really about. Many statements simply pass by almost unnoticed while others that apparently arouse widespread support – like "industrial democracy is what we need" – turn out to mean very different things to different people.

In this book we have suggested two ways of introducing some system into the debate so that a real exchange of opinion may take place. First a distinction should be made between the various goals – economic, social etc – and the practical measures suggested for their achievement. Secondly an attempt should be made to apply scientific knowledge about the functioning of industrial organizations to an analysis of relations between means and ends.

Our main task has been to try to compile at least part of such a theory. We have devoted five out of eight chapters to this end. The most important lines in the theory have already been summarized; the preceding chapter contained an attempt at applying it.

We have shown how the theory can be used in forecasting the possible reactions of management and the trade unions to the discussion of industrial democracy. Furthermore we tried somewhat tentatively to use the theory in an analysis of the relations between ends and means – something that seems to us of great importance. First we specified the goals (ideology). It appeared that several factors, commonly regarded as quite distinct, in fact bore some relation to one another. Two objectives in particular seemed to provide the link:

1. To find ways of satisfactorily balancing the different interests in the company.
2. To find methods of production and management that will lead to high productivity, thus enabling the company to satisfy the demands made on it by the stakeholders. At the same time the concept of productivity nees redefining.

The next step was naturally to examine the practical program. How far are the goals already being achieved? What are the most striking weaknesses? What parts of the practical program seem best adapted to achieving the goals?

We, like all other researchers in this field, have been hampered by the incompleteness of the available theories and by the lack of empirical tests. Thus, whilst our attempt to answer the questions posed has been based partly on the theory presented, it also of necessity included much subjective evaluation and judgment.

Many of our views have been rather critical of several common practices of industrial democracy. At the same time we are far from implying that the whole debate to date can be written off as unimportant.

"INDUSTRIAL DEMOCRACY" – A USEFUL CONCEPT?

Our attempts to specify goals and reformulate some of the problems usually connected with "industrial democracy" highlighted another question: is this concept really meaningful? Before attempting an answer, let us first take another look at the difficulty of even trying to define accurately what is usually meant by the term.

Earlier in the book we begged the question by saying simply that "industrial democracy" is "what people mean when they say they are discussing industrial democracy". In so far as our analysis has been a development of this definition, it has shown fairly convincingly that people are referring to different things, albeit under the same name.

This lack of precision is confusing but hardly unique. The social sciences in particular have often had to deal with similarly diffuse and vaguely defined problems. It may even be an advantage that the debate has included no attempt at producing a precise definition. After all, in many spheres the research of the last ten years has been concerned to show that earlier definitions were unsuitable. This has happened in psychiatry and medicine where the boundary previously fixed between physical and mental illness has proved increasingly untenable. Again in sociology and political sciences the relations between the legal system and general cultural systems have proved just as complex; and now in organization theory we find it difficult to distinguish between the social, economic and technical problems.

On the other hand, one may well wonder whether a label should really be attached to something so ill-defined. A rubric like "industrial democracy" can create more problems than it solves. Such battlecries can do valuable work in catching attention, but they can also lead to confusion, giving rise to expectations that cannot be fulfilled.

For instance, is there any point in an isolated discussion of problems involving the relations between individuals or groups in the restricted environment known as the "place of work"? Life in the company is not isolated. On the contrary it is connected in a multitude of ways to life outside, probably making it very difficult to influence conditions within the company without changing external conditions too. In a rural factory the status system, for instance, can hardly be changed without radically altering the whole surrounding community. Furthermore, social conditions in the community are highly dependent on the norms, traditions, social conditions etc of the rest of the country, and even, in the case of Sweden, of Scandinavia, Western Europe and the whole of the western world. The way in which the foreman and the workers in the factory or the president and the chief engineer conceive the relation between superior and subordinate is probably just as affected by their experiences in everyday life as it is by conditions in the company. Nor can changes in the company's status system be seen in isolation; they are simply part of a network which might include, for example, technical and economic development, changes in administrative techniques or new openings for trading.

It also seems important to remember that the debate on industrial democracy – despite its bold rallying cry – has not introduced any very specialized questions or any problems that have suffered previous neglect. Managers can point out quite truthfully that from their point of view the debate has been concerned with some methods – perhaps not even particularly remarkable ones – of achieving higher productivity and good relations with the employees (goals that have always been thought essential). And the employees can state that it has simply been a question of some new weapons – some of dubious value – in the old struggle to uphold their interests in the company.

If the term "industrial democracy", overloaded with time-worn emotions and evaluations, is abandoned, all parties may be able to devote more time and effort to examining and specifying the goals. When they then come to considering methods, they should feel less tied to the "traditional" prescriptions.

We should perhaps repeat that none of these comments is intended to belittle the importance of the questions discussed. What we have already said several times still applies: not only are these matters topical, they are also of great importance to us all, employees, customers, business leaders, owners, politicians or researchers. Our intention has rather been to appeal for a broader view with less dependence on a possible antiquated program of action.

TWO FURTHER COMMENTS

In this final chapter we may usefully underline two other conclusions, or at any rate reflections, which we have touched upon before.

To begin with we must be on our guard against expecting too much, of hoping for final solutions to the problems of "industrial democracy". It has often been pointed out that social problems have no ultimate solution. The reader cannot have failed to notice in the foregoing analysis that there seem to be arguments both for and against most of the various practical prescriptions. This is not surprising. It is a pretty good reflection of real life. Most measures are likely to have bad sides as well as good ones. And when we remember all the demands for greater freedom, security, satisfaction, productivity etc., it would be rather surprising to find a practical program which could realize all the goals simultaneously.

Despite all this it is easy to fall into wishful thinking and it is therefore important to remember the many reservations made by us and by others. It cannot, for instance, be taken for granted that increased employee influence leads to greater satisfaction or higher productivity; only under very special circumstances can one expect the majority of employees to have the chance or the interest to make a constructive contribution to the really important and complicated decision-making in the company. The consequences of increasing specialization are unlikely to be more than slightly counterbalanced by even the most ambitious joint-consultation program. The most successful suggestions schemes, for example, have been shown to be of little economic value compared with the efficiency improvements introduced by trained experts. And this problem is by no means restricted to the rank and file: many professional business leaders regard the Board of Directors as a body fit to handle only fairly insignificant problems, since their limited technical knowledge could lead to unfortunate decisions.

The second comment is this: it is naturally difficult to find general prescriptions for the problems discussed here. We have mentioned repeatedly that the success of any managerial method or the suitability of any type of organization will depend on the individual company's circumstances. The same is probably true in the sphere of industrial democracy. The most effective solutions will be those that are best adapted to the individual company's technical, economic, organizational, geographical, social and psychological conditions. And not only this: inside the company, too, are important differences which should not be forgotten. Different groups or categories may often, for instance, be working in very different environments. That these differences are usually ignored has recently been pointed out as a main reason for many organizational and administrative difficulties.

What, after all, is "democratic" about refusing to admit the very different conditions in the maintenance and the production departments; or that leadership style may decisively affect the employees' way of understanding, for example, a consultative committee; or that the social environment of the local bank in a small town does not have much in common with the environment of the head office in the big city?

Organization experts have raised a demand for "differentiated management"; "differentiated democracy" would almost certainly have a much greater chance of success than any simple, general solutions embodied in central agreements or general legislation.

We are only too aware that this presentation suffers from many weaknesses. To conclude, here are some of the points most open to serious objection.

Many concepts are still horrifyingly ill defined. All too often they are expressed in non-operational terms, i.e. without being directly related to a method of measurement. Any propositions automatically inherit the uncertainty of the concepts. Furthermore, the propositions are generally qualitative rather than quantitative. And the lack of empirical material is serious. Other propositions can easily be regarded as truisms. Often the choice of terms could be criticized and the reader may sometimes wonder if all the new terms are really necessary.

An almost unavoidable problem is that theories, and empirical material even more so, tend to refer to situations already rendered out-of-date by economic, social and technical development. Examples can easily be found. Some have already been mentioned in other chapters.

Current changes in the quality and quantity of the working population of industry indicate that many of the future problems of industrial democracy will be concerned with the white-collar group. The great majority of all empirical material in industrial sociology is concerned with the workers in production. If many of the results of leadership research already seem out-of-date, this is because educational conditions and continuous specialization are changing the boss-subordinate relationship; quite often nowadays, for example, the subordinate is more competent within a specialized area, than his boss. This and other technical changes make life continually more difficult for an organization which, in theory, is based on a hierarchical structure. The trend towards what is called "management automation" envisages machines as organization members in quite new roles and involves radical changes in many leadership roles. Rapid changes in the company's environment continually raise new problems of adjustment. The divorce between ownership rights and leadership continues at an accelerating speed. The educational and social background of business leaders is changing.

The conclusion must be that we can scarcely base our considerations on the conditions of yesterday or even today. It is most important to think ahead to future conditions.

However, it is not the only weakness of the empirical material that it relates to a time which already differs essentially from our own. By far the major part of it comes also from an environment different from ours. On several points it seems that the differences between North America and the Scandinavian countries are so great as to render American research of very limited general value. And most of our material does in fact come from the United States.

Perhaps the most serious weakness of all is the uncertainty of some of the fundamental assumptions on which the discussion is based. Most important is probably that throughout this book, with few exceptions, the individual and the company have been treated as homogeneous concepts – the assumption that one person is the same as another; that it is possible to make generalizations about the individual's needs and reactions etc. These are usual but embarrassingly uncertain prerequisites. In many instances we have made the equally doubtful assumption that one company is the same as another. On account of varying size, production techniques, markets and history, the needs and possibilities of companies vary widely; so too will the effects of any particular action and the way in which different actions are interpreted. One of the most serious consequences of such simplifications is that they cloud the real difficulties involved in generalizing about the effects of various practical measures. The only defence we can plead is that the theory available unfortunately constrains us to make some unrealistic assumptions.

NEED FOR RESEARCH

What we have presented in these pages is a tentative theory rather than a fully developed and empirically tested one. We could say that we have made suggestions for drawing maps but have not provided a set of complete charts. It is therefore important to devote a few lines to the question of further research.

As we have seen, important advances in the fundamental theories have been made during the last few years. The theory of company goals owes its development mainly to a fruitful interplay between economic and sociological theory on the one hand and general systems theory on the other. Modern conflict theory has been much inspired by the fundamental concepts of game theory. Leadership research, which a few years ago seemed to have reached a dead end, has been stimulated by new results from research concerning small groups. The examples could easily be multiplied.

Such basic research must be stimulated and supported. This can hardly be overemphasized. Take almost any branch of specialized research, for instance in personnel administration, and what do we find? Success up to now has undoubtedly been hampered and useful paths obstructed by the lack of fundamental theories.

It is characteristic of many of the new theories that they have resulted from cooperation between the established disciplines. Many consider that this trend will be still more marked in the future. Even more than at present research will involve teamwork. Unfortunately it is likely that projects will consequently be big and costly and difficult to fit into the established scientific institutions.

Obviously it is not possible in the bulk of fundamental research to distinguish particular projects specifically concerned with the problems of industrial democracy. It will rather be a question of obtaining some general knowledge about the functioning of organizations and their interplay with the environment.

But fundamental research alone is not enough. The results so far obtained, some of which have been mentioned in this book, need to be followed up and developed. We can mention here a few of the things that could probably be achieved by such development work within the foreseeable future.

In Scandinavia research institutes and industry itself have devoted large resources to developing more efficient and hygienic working methods. "Hygiene" has successively taken on a new and wider meaning. This reflects the growing demands made on the company by the employees and by society. It can only be regarded as a very promising trend that companies and researchers have set their sights even higher in this respect. The best known example and most comprehensive program is provided by the Anglo-Norwegian research team mentioned in a previous chapter. Its purpose is to reconstruct the socio-technical system of the place of work in such a way that the employees can better satisfy their basic needs while productivity is maintained or even increased. A few companies in Sweden have already shown some interest in similar experiments.

Bolder experiments in consultation procedures have been called for in

Sweden and some have even been undertaken, mainly within the framework of the joint consultation committee system. We gladly support this call. It can be questioned, however, whether experiments should be restricted to these committees. There is much evidence of a need for bold experimentation in general industrial management. It is probable, after all, that the chances of achieving success through consultation are highly dependent on such factors as the training of managers and supervisors, the basic rules for decision-making codified in the company policy, the wage system and the methods of long-range planning.

Unfortunately many a good idea has earned a bad reputation because its enthusiastic supporters have presented it as a cure-all. It seems clear that there are no such magic solutions. Most of these "inventions" have favorable sides, but have other consequences which from various points of view may be less desirable. This is no unique situation. Similar difficulties have not prevented us from grabbing eagerly at the technical developments made possible by exploiting advances in the natural sciences.

NOTES AND COMMENTS

Chapter 1

p. 1
Résumés of the industrial democracy debate and concrete examples of the various programs suggested or tried out in different countries, can be found in The Problems of Industrial Democracy (Den industriella demokratins problem, 1923), Dale (1949), Newman (1955), Clegg (1960) and The Trade Union Movement and Industrial Democracy (Fackföreningsrörelsen och företagsdemokratin, 1961) etc. For descriptions of management-employee cooperation in Swedish companies, see Göransson (1927), Westerlund (1951), Smith (1961) and others.

pp. 6–8
Wärneryd (1959), McGregor (1960) and others have discussed in popular form the place of scientific theory in a debate of this type.

p. 8
Fayol (1916) and Gulick & Urwick (1937) are two leading writers on classical administration theory. Comparisons between this theory and the human relations movement have been made by March & Simon (1958), Krupp (1961) and others. There will be further reference to writers concerned with the human relations movement in notes and comments, chapter 5.

pp. 9–11
Among the many comparisons between past organizations and large modern business enterprises, the following are of particular interest: Drucker (1950), Boulding (1954), Cordiner (1956), Berle (1960) and Mason (1960).

pp. 10–11
The terms *company* and *organization* frequently appear in this study. They should not of course be regarded as synonyms, since in everyday usage a company is taken to be a type of organization. I have not defined these concepts more clearly, partly because it seems to me that the basic differences between various kinds of organizations are quite different from those usually suggested. Thus I share in the main the view of the American economist Boulding, as expressed in the following passage:

It becomes harder and harder to tell nasty, moneygrubbing corporations from virtuous, non-profit institutions. Indeed, I suspect sometimes that a type of organization called the not-very-profit organization is going to gobble us all up. The university, the research corporation, the hospital, the mutual insurance company, and the cooperative all seem to be moving toward profit making while the plain old money-making corporation moves in the direction of good works, contributions to the Community Chest, support of universities, allotments to pensions, welfare funds and Christmas turkeys. Pretty soon it is going to be hard to tell General Motors from the Salvation Army. (Boulding, 1963)

However, the reader should also refer to chapter 8, where the need for a more detailed analysis of the differences between companies is emphasized.

pp. 10–11

For some of the differences between organizations see, for example, Etzioni (1961).

p. 11

Since the theory that a scientific writer chooses as his starting-point will greatly affect his subsequent choice among the available subject matter, much of the space in scientific studies is usually devoted to reporting on what the author has decided to leave out. This work contains no such specific survey, mainly because there would be practically no end to it. The subject discussed here is extremely comprehensive and has engaged many scientific disciplines, for example economics, sociology, social psychology and political science. I have tried here to restrict myself consistently to the more or less generally accepted approach of the discipline that is evolving somewhere half-way between economics and sociology, usually known as organization theory.

Chapter 2

p. 14

The idea that owners and management exert the influence while the employees are powerless, has its counterpart in economic theory. For a criticism of this view, see Galbraith (1952).

An account of the German legislation on employee representation is to be found in Clegg (1960). The suggestion that management committees should be transformed into staff organs is also made in The Trade Union Movement and Industrial Democracy (Fackföreningsrörelsen och företagsdemokratin, 1961).

p. 15

The Glacier Metal experiment has been described by Jaques (1951) and Brown (1960). There is some similarity between this experiment and some that have been made in Scandinavia – for example at Volvo-Skövde – which involve a considerable extension of the work of the management committees. See Söderström & Rodert (1962). The reader can obtain a picture of recent development in the theory of company goals from Frenckner (1953) and Boulding (1954). Important contributions have also been made by Barnard (1938), Brady (1943), Simon (1947), Dahl & Lindblom (1953) and Selznick (1957).

pp. 16–17
Rhenman (1964b) cites several quotations to show that the term "goal" can mean quite different things to different writers. Neumann & Morgenstern (1947) and Baumol (1959) are well known among those who have tried to develop an economic theory based on different assumptions from the traditional one of profit maximization. Fältström & Sparr (1959) give some idea of how Scandinavian companies interpret the concept of company policy. The literature of classical organization theory (e.g. Newman, 1951 and Koontz & O'Donnell, 1959) serves to supplement their picture.

pp. 17–18
Ericsson (1960) discusses the goals and policy of a Scandinavian company. He also mentions some of the reasons why management may consider a codified company policy desirable.

pp. 18–19
A résumé of the way in which the concept of organizational goals is handled in sociological theory can be found in Johnson (1960).

The sociological concept of function is discussed by Merton (1957) and others.

pp. 18–20
The relation between the goal of the organization, the way the goal is conceived by the individual decision-maker and the goals prescribed by management is discussed more fully in Rhenman (1964b). For other analyses of the goal concept, see for example, March & Simon (1958) and Marples (1960). Leibenstein (1960) and Cyert & March (1963) argue convincingly, that any explanation of company behavior in an economic theory should be preceded by studies of the company's organization and its individual decision-makers.

pp. 20–21
According to the definitions given here, goals refer to the desired consequences of behavior, while norms and plans are direct expression of desired behavior. In order to render these definitions operational – for example so that we can classify rules of behavior into these categories in an empirical study – it will be necessary to relate the concepts to a definite description level, i.e. to indicate the terms in which a particular individual's behavior can be described. Otherwise it is impossible to avoid complications arising from the fact that goals, norms and plans often form a hierarchy and that what in one context is a goal is, in another, a norm or a plan.

pp. 21–22
For a description of the means-end hierarchy, i.e. the network of goals, norms and

plans in a company, the reader is referred to Barnard (1938) and Simon (1947). Writers have customarily referred to the hierarchy of superior and inferior goals as main goals and subgoals. See, for example, Frenckner (1953).

p. 23
There have been several empirical investigations of the various conceptions of goals and norms found in an organization. That of Gouldner (1954) is particularly interesting since it includes a picture of how the conceptions change and what the changes mean to the organization.

Consultants who have studied company organizations often mention disagreement in the conceptions of goals, norms and plans as a common weakness (cf. Drucker, 1954 and Carlberg, 1961). A main cause of this lack of agreement is the selectivity of the perceptions of the individuals. For instance a person's earlier experiences will greatly influence the way in which he perceives concrete situations. For an experiment illustrating this phenomenon, see Dearborn & Simon (1958).

Another major group of behavior rules, not discussed in this chapter, is connected with the allocation of roles. Cf. notes and comments on chapters 4 and 5. A résumé of sociological role theory, and a fuller analysis, can be found in Gross, Mason & McEachern (1958).

p. 23
The expression "clear goals and norms" has been used here, although it is one of the most equivocal terms in the whole of organization theory. That an organization member has received "a clear message", and thus has a "clear idea" of it, seems to mean either:
that he has received a message which is understandable
that he has received a message that is reliable
that he has received a message that does not contradict other simultaneous or earlier messages, or
that he has received a message in sufficient detail for him to act upon.

p. 23
For a discussion of the relation between congruence in the goal conceptions of the organization members and the existence of conflict, the reader is referred to Rhenman, Strömberg & Westerlund (1963).

p. 24
In the main, the theory developed here links up with Barnard and Simon's theory of organizational equilibrium (inducement and contribution). A full account of this theory and a number of illustrated examples can be found in Simon, Smithburgh & Thompson (1950). However, the present discussion constitutes an extension and a more precise definition of the theory, influenced by modern conflict theory. A similar general approach has also been suggested by Carlson, Höglund & Söderman (1952).

pp. 24-26
Barnard (1958) has discussed management's dependence on general social norms. More recent sociological research has devoted much attention to the norms and evaluations that characterize the business world as a sub-culture. However, countries differ so greatly in this respect that American research results, for example, will have very little to offer the student of Scandinavian conditions. Cf. for example Warner & Mattin (1959, especially chapter 9) and Browaldh (1961). An interesting comparison between managers and management in different countries has been made by Granick (1960 and 1962).

Among studies that illustrate the dependence of management on the company's stakeholders are Selznick (1949), Höglund (1953) and Brown (1960).

That conflicts of interest between owners and management have also been paid some attention in normative business economic literature can be seen from Donaldson (1963).

The theory of company goals has been illustrated indirectly in the memoirs of many business leaders. See, for example, Sloan (1941) and Girdler (1943).

pp. 25-27
The factors that decide whether employees stay with a company have been the subject of many studies. A review of some of these works can be found in March & Simon (1958). An interesting theory of staff turnover has also been outlined by Hedberg (1963).

pp. 26-27
Roberts (1956 and 1958) and Simon (1957b) have both made important contributions to the discussion of what influences management remuneration.

Another factor that might explain Carlson's simile (Carlson, 1951) in which management is compared to a puppet, is the phenomenon usually known as Gresham's law, i.e. the tendency for many small tasks to fritter away the working day, leaving no time for more important matters.

pp. 27-28
A more specified picture of management's motives is provided by Katona (1951) and Bendix (1956). Thompson & McEwen (1958) report empirical studies showing that the demands of the different parties can be so contradictory as to make survival practically impossible.

For a discussion of the relations between management and owners in an economy characterized by professional business management and scattered ownership, see Berle (1960) and Mason (1959).

Stagner (1956) quotes a strike at General Electric as an example of cooperation between employees and customers.

p. 27-28
Selznick (1957) is one of the few authors who has really penetrated the question of leadership types in the sense used here. The material available to him was, however, rather one-sided and he has therefore relied among other things on historical comparisons. Thus he also considers it possible to find among political leaders examples of a very clear formulation of the "mission of the organization" being combined with the belief that leadership must be anchored in the demands and needs of the stakeholders. Leys (1962) believes that both types of leadership discussed in this chapter can be traced back to two main trends in Western leadership philosophy, namely Platonism and Macchiavellianism.

Riesman (1954), Bendix (1956) and Whyte (1956) have put forward different theories as to how new social norms have affected the selection of business managers.

pp. 28-30
Our description of management's problem-solving technique can be traced back in the main to March & Simon (1958). On the subject of the means-end analysis, see also Rhenman (1964a). As regards the state of "natural inaction", it should perhaps be added that this is recognized as a serious problem in many companies and the establishment of research and development departments – e.g. product development, production technique, market research, industrial engineering etc. – can be seen as a conscious effort to combat the tendency. A theory of management behavior in situations where it is possible to satisfy the demands of all the stakeholders without difficulty has been suggested by Cyert & March (1963) in their propositions about organizational slack.

p. 30
The interpretation of the profit-maximizing goal suggested here, does not agree with all economists' opinions on the matter. Cf. for example, Simon (1957). A more usual formulation is that profit is the company's main goal but that there are other subgoals too, or that the company pursues the main goal under certain restrictions. Cf., for example Chamberlain (1962). Chamberlain, however, devotes a great deal of attention to conditions inside the company, planning methods, decision-making etc. For other relevant examples of economists' assumptions about company goals, see Krelle (1961).

Chapter 3

p. 33
The cry of doom has also been raised by other authors, for example Moreno (1934) and Menninger (1938). The efforts of the human relations movement to abolish conflict and create some sort of harmony are reflected by Mayo (1945), Foulkes & Anthony (1957) and others. For a criticism of this attitude see, for example, Riesman (1954) and Whyte (1956). The pioneers of the scientific management movement believed that conflict between employer and employees could be solved by scientific analysis (see, for example, Taylor, 1947).

p. 35
The following works together can provide a picture of the development of conflict theory: Neumann & Morgenstern (1947), Lewin (1948), Coser (1956), Sherif & Sherif (1956) and Richardson (1959). Modern conflict research has received much stimulus from an interest in political and military conflicts. (See Schelling, 1960; Boulding, 1962 and The Journal of Conflict Resolution.) An important contribution to the treatment of conflict in management theory was made by Metcalf & Urwick (1941).

p. 36
Our basic theory and concepts can in the main be traced back to Ackoff (1962) and Boulding (1962). What we have here called conflicts of interest have sometimes been called by other writers "competition" (cf. Deutsch, 1949). However, it seems to me that this term could well be misleading in view of its other widely accepted usage in economics.

A theory of aspiration level can be found in March & Simon (1958). Cf. also Lewin et.al. (1944).

A fuller theory would have to distinguish between "objective conflicts of interest" and the conceptions of the parties concerned of the conflict situation – "subjective conflicts of interest". I shall not make this distinction here.

pp. 37-38
The difference between various states of conflicts has been analyzed by Rapoport (1961).

pp. 39-44
Our outline of a theory of institutions for conflict resolution owes most to Stagner (1956) and Thompson & McEwen (1958). A theory of coöptation has been suggested by Selznick (1949). A theory of coalition between the stakeholders of an organization can be found in Cyert & March (1959). Something similar to joint decision-making and coöptation has been described by Gouldner (1954). Gouldner introduces the concept of "boundary roles" to refer to persons whose task it is to resolve conflicts between a stakeholder and the organization.

p. 40-44
Clegg (1960) briefly discusses some of the analyses of the democracy concept to be found in the political sciences and compares systems of representation with other methods of resolving conflict between group interests. In the present work I have not discussed the concept of democracy as it is viewed in the literature of the political scientists.

p. 42
Classical economic theory has of course described situations involving joint decision-making (e.g. oligopoly) but has not got very far in analyzing the factors that affect the parties' chances of upholding their interests. This theory has therefore not been discussed here (cf. Harsanyi, 1956). Our breakdown of the decision process has been based mainly

on decision theory. Bross (1953) provides a convenient introduction. In political science other grounds for classification have also been suggested (cf., for example, Lasswell & Kaplan, 1950 and Lasswell, 1956). Edwards (1954 and 1961) provides a survey of psychological models of decision-making.

p. 43
The classification into types of conflict has been taken from Rhenman, Strömberg & Westerlund (1963) with only a slight alteration in terminology.

p. 44
The analysis of factors affecting the influence of the parties has been based, in the main, on Schelling (1960).

p. 45
There are also illegitimate rewards, such as bribes etc.

p. 48
An analysis of social norms affecting the outcome of negotiations between employee and employer can be found in Wootton (1955) and Fürstenberg (1958).

p. 50
Two well-known works, which reflect the optimistic hope that social psychological research could abolish conflict, are Kornhauser, Dubin & Ross (1954) and Stagner (1956).

A more pessimistic attitude can be found in Blumer (1954) and Baldamus (1961).

pp. 50–52
Our discussion on the effects of conflict owes much to Coser (1954) and Dubin (1961)

pp. 52–53
The "scapegoat" theory reoccurs in several works, for example, Weber (1947) and Jaques (1951).

Chapter 4

p. 56
Clegg (1960) analyses institutional conditions in different countries. The material on the attitude of the British trade unions can be found in Clegg and elsewhere.

p. 58
The definitions of staff and line positions, as they appear in classical organization theory, have been discussed by Sagen (1958). Carlson, Höglund & Söderman (1952) consider that, under the present Swedish agreement, the management committees can already be regarded as a staff organ. Examples of committees of various kinds being incorporated in the organization charts of large companies are given by Holden, Fish & Smith (1941) and Stieglitz (1961).

p. 59
Unfortunately few detailed studies of decision-making in companiee have been made. An interesting and fairly comprehensive practical study has been presented by Cyert, Simon & Trow (1956). See also Wärneryd (1957) and Strömberg & Wirdenius (1961). For a theoretical analysis of decision-making, see Thrall, Coombs & Davies (1954), Simon (1960) and the literature referred to in the comments on chapter 3.

p. 60
Readers interested in group problem-solving, with a view to studying the possibility of a successful use of management committees in problem-solving, are referred to Shaw (1932), Thorndyke (1938), McCurdy & Lambert (1951/52), Kelley & Thibaut (1954), Schmidt & Buchanan (1954) and Torrance (1956/57).

In chapter 5 we discuss the relation between the company's technology and the possibility of engaging the employees in problem-solving.

pp. 64-65
Decentralization, i.e. the transfer of the right of final decision to subordinate managers, can perhaps be regarded as a democratic measure. For a discussion of factors affecting the possibility of decentralization, see Drucker (1946), Dale (1952), Simon, Smithburg & Thompson (1950) and Kruisinga (1954). The influence of information technology on the trend towards decentralization is discussed in chapter 6.

There are some authors who claim that the absorption of uncertainty in connection with decision-making is important, in particular by affecting the status of the individual. Cf., Jaques (1951) and Crozier (1963). However, the value of the results of their research is considerably reduced by the primitive models of the decision process that they use.

p. 65
For an analysis of the concept of responsibility, see Dimock (1960).

pp. 66-67
The view of authority in classical organization theory is illustrated, for example, by Mooney (1947).

pp. 67-69
The theory of authority suggested here represents in the main a combination of the basic ideas of Barnard (1938) and Weber (1947). Similar attempts at a synthesis have been made by Presthus (1958), Hopkins (1961) and others.

Ahlmann & Rhenman (1964) show that every theory of authority must be based on a fundamental theory of the individual organization member. An example of a theory of authority deduced from simple postulates about the individual is that suggested by Homans (1961)

p. 68
Blau (1955) and many others have shown that a leader's authority depends on his behavior. Brown (1960) makes an interesting contribution to the industrial democracy debate with an analysis of ways in which the authority of management can be legitimatized.

pp. 69–71
The classical work on the status system in organizations is Barnard (1946). Bass (1960) can represent those who have tried to combine the available research results into an integrated theory.

Chapter 5

pp. 75–77
Cf. also The Post-war Program of the Labor Movement (Arbetarrörelsens efterkrigsprogram, 1944), where it is stated that "workers, both manual and non-manual, must have the opportunity of influencing technical and economic working conditions so as to increase both security and satisfaction at work and the ability of the companies to provide remuneration" (our translation)

pp. 77–79
For further details of the pioneers of the scientific management movement and their attitude to these questions, see Taylor (1947), Gantt (1916) and Gilbreth & Gilbreth (1918).

p. 80
For a résumé of research into fatigue, see Homans (1941) and Ryan (1947). The experiments at Western Electric have been most fully described by Roethlisberger & Dickson (1939).

An example of how some prominent members of the human-relations movement have evaluated the scientific management movement is provided by Katz & Kahn (1951).

pp. 80–81
For some criticism of the Western Electric experiments, see Miller & Form (1951), Boalt & Westerlund (1953) and Landsberger (1958).

There have been many attempts at an impartial evaluation of the human-relations movement. Some relevant contributions have been made, for example, by MacKinzie (1952), Shepard (1956), Knowles (1958), Bennis (1959), Koontz (1961) and Krupp (1961).

Information systems in Swedish companies have been studied by Dahlström (1956).

p. 81
For a recent survey of leadership research, see Likert (1961). For a discussion of research on general management problems, see March & Simon (1958).

pp. 82
A résumé of earlier research into types of leaders is provided by Jenkins (1947) and Stogdill (1948).

The democratic and authoritarian leadership styles were first defined by Lewin (1944). Some well-known studies, in which different leadership styles are compared, are: Lewin, Lippit & White (1939), Coch & French (1948), Westerlund (1952) and Kahn & Katz (1953). For a survey of the literature that discusses the relation between leadership and productivity, see Jennings (1958).

There have been many studies demonstrating that a democratic leadership is not necessarily to be preferred from the point of view of productivity. Some of these are: Bos (1937), Comry, Pfiffner & High (1954), Fleishman, Harris & Burtt (1955), Morse & Reimer (1956) and Blau & Scott (1962).

p. 83
Several studies demonstrate that high morale and high productivity are not necessarily correlated. Examples are: Mossin (1949) and Fleishman, Harris & Burtt (1955), Brayfield & Crockett (1955), Jennings (1958) and Likert (1961) provide surveys of the literature; they all come to the conclusion that there is no simple relation between morale and productivity.

pp. 84-85
Various writers have suggested factors which, alongside those included in the concepts of democractic and authoritarian leadership, can be expected to have some effect on productivity. Examples are: High level of ambition (Blau & Scott, 1962), social distance (Fiedler, 1957), consistent behavior (Comrey, Pfiffner & High, 1954), independence vis-à-vis superiors (Pelz, 1952) and superior technical skill (Pfiffner, 1955).

One of the earliest contributions to the study of leadership in different situations was Hemphill (1949). This work concentrated mainly on what can be called the "internal" leadership situation, i.e. the characteristics of the follower, both as a group and as an individual. Hansson (1962) adds a contribution of his own and makes a comparison between some other studies with this focus of interest. Features of the "external" leadership situation, which are thought to be of importance to the success of the leadership, are such things as the personalities of the follower (Jennings, 1958), the attitude of the top leaders and the character of the tasks (Fleishman, Harris & Burtt, 1955) and the general social environment (Brayfield & Crockett, 1955).

Surveys of the literature have been provided by Härnqvist (1956) and Likert (1961).

pp. 85-88
Another example of the effect of work demands on leadership style is provided by Coser (1958). For a general discussion of the effect of technology on management, see Thompson & Bates (1957).

For studies of assembly-line production, see Walker & Guest (1952) and Walker, Guest & Turner (1956).

For the effect of automation on working conditions see, for example, Walker (1957) and Simpson (1959).

pp. 88-89
The Tavistock studies and their theoretical background have been described by Rice (1958).

The best known and most comprehensive experiments on job-enlargement have been carried out by Lincoln Industries under the leadership of the company's founder and president (Lincoln, 1946 and 1951). Another practical case has been described by Richardson & Walker (1948).

In many companies individual work study engineers have carried out experiments of their own. The type of theory from which they have generally started has been illustrated by Davis & Canter (1955) and Davis (1957).

pp. 90-91
Westerlund (1958) has discussed some of the measurement problems connected with the productivity concept and has pointed out the lack of correlation between different productivity concepts and the absence of systematic reliability tests.

For a general résumé of the productivity concept from points of view other than those applied here, see Ruist (1960).

For a criticism of the "numerator" in the productivity concept, see Likert (1961). For a criticism of the "denominator", see Baldamus (1951).

p. 91
As an alternative to reformulating the productivity concept, it could be assumed that it is not possible to evaluate the group or organization unit solely on the basis of its productivity (measured in the conventional way). This has been suggested by Stogdill (1959) and others. Stogdill summarizes his conclusions as follows:
This book was undertaken with the aim of developing an adequate theory of group achievement. The author has not found it possible to construct a logically consistent theory based on the hypothesis that productivity is the only achievement of organization. A great deal of work with a variety of charts, tables, diagrams, equations, and

symbolic models was performed in order to arrive at a satisfactory solution. The first models were constructed in terms of the prevailing theories, with performance and interaction as inputs; with expectations, role structure, group integration, and morale as intervening variables; and with productivity as the output. These models failed not only to exhibit any internal consistency but also to account for the experimental findings. ...

It is therefore proposed that the essential dimensions of organization achievement are *productivity, morale, and integration.* The input variables and the group structures and operational mechanics necessary to generate these outcomes have been described in the preceding chapters. Group *productivity* is defined as the degree of change in expectancy values created by the group operations. Group *integration* is defined as the extent to which structure and operations are capable of being maintained under stress. Group *morale* is defined as degree of freedom from restraint in action toward a goal.

Chapter 6

p. 93
Fleishman, Harris & Burtt (1955) have demonstrated the effect of the superiors on the likelihood of a subordinate manager's succeeding with a particular leadership style.

pp. 93–94
For a discussion on the relation between information technology and demands at different levels of the managerial hierarchy, the reader is referred to Ackoff (1955), Leavitt & Whisler (1958) and Anshen (1960).

pp. 94–100
There is no great difference between Weber's view of leadership in an organization (cf. Weber, 1947) and that of classical organization theory (e.g. Fayol, 1916, or Mooney, 1947). As regards the view of authority, the reader is referred to the notes and comments on chapter 4

pp. 95–100
For an interesting anthropological comparison of authority relations in different cultures, see Miller (1959).

A discussion of the line-staff principle and its historical background can be found in Rhenman, Strömberg & Westerlund (1963).

The concept of informal organization probably dates back at least to Durkheim (1932). As regards the Western Electric studies, see references in the previous chapter.

p. 98
The influence of language on perception is discussed in Hayakawa (1952); a criticism of the tendency towards dichotomies and simple classifications can also be found there.

pp. 98 – 99
The need for horizontal contacts has been studied by Simpson (1959), Landsberger (1961) and others. For a discussion of joint decision-making, see March & Simon (1958) and Rhenman, Strömberg & Westerlund (1963). Thompson (1961) has discussed the problems arising from the increasingly common situation in modern organizations, namely that the competence of the subordinates is greater than that of their superiors.

pp. 99–101
On the functions of leadership, see Barnard (1938), Simon (1947), Knickerbocker (1948), Selznick (1957), Parsons (1958), Bennis (1959) and others.

pp. 99–100
The difference between retaining the employees in the organization unit and stimulating them to maximum performance is discussed by Katz & Kahn (1952), Brayfield & Crockett (1955), March & Simon (1958), Herzberg, Mausner & Snyderman (1959) and others.

p. 100
The rivalry between organization units is described by Dalton (1959), Dimock (1960), Janowitz (1960) and others.

It cannot be assumed that leadership has functional consequences only. The status differential, which seems to be an inevitable consequence of individual leadership, can constitute among other things, an obstacle to efficient communications and problem-solving.

pp. 101–102
A discussion of program control (which corresponds more or less to briefing), can be found in March & Simon (1958) and Rhenman (1966).

Blau (1955) describes the behavior of a leader seeking access to informal sanctions and power. Drucker (1954) and McGregor (1960) discuss the question of leadership in situations where the leader and the follower are dependent on each other. The influences at work on those who make decisions and solve problems have been discussed by Simon (1947) and others.

Control by means of the technical environment is discussed by Richardson & Walker (1948), Woodward (1958) and others.

pp. 103–104
Benne & Sheats (1948), Knickerbocker (1948), Bales & Slater (1955) and others have discussed the idea that the different functions of leadership can be exercized by different members of the group.

The informal organization and the group norms can be regarded as a kind of self-government. Their genesis has been discussed above.

For decision-making in organizations, see references in chapter 4.

Studies of the relation between "clear organization" and the probability of success in different environments, have been made by Burns & Stalker (1961).

pp. 104-106
It is a popular but false belief that first a goal is set and then plans to achieve the goal worked out. This matter has been discussed further in Rhenman (1964a).

The whole question of how subordinates feel about their boss' right of decision is very complex. They probably react sharply to anything that might appear high-handed. On the other hand empirical studies have shown that a manager has a better chance of influencing his subordinates if he can show himself in some degree independent of his own superiors. Cf. Pelz (1952).

For some interpretations of the role of boss which, in the main, link up with those suggested here, the reader is referred to Drucker (1954), McMurry (1958), Argyris (1960), Likert (1961) and McGregor (1960).

Blau & Scott (1962) discuss the relation between technological developments and the possibility of creating a more favorable work environment. Cf. also Mann & Williams (1960) and Mann & Hoffmann (1960).

Chapter 7

p. 110
For a discussion of the concept of egoistic needs, based on a theory of motivation, see Maslow (1954).

The reader can probably best get some idea of the complicated nature of the techniques of management and administration by studying the seminar programs for business managers arranged by various institutions. See, for example, the programs offered by the American Management Association.

p. 112
Among businessmen who have been pioneers in trying out various democratic measures can be mentioned Walpole (1944), Renold (1950) and Brown (1960). Swedish businessmen interested in such matters have rarely published their experiences.

Modern administrative techniques include a great many methods for conveying information from management to employees, but very few for conveying it in the other direction.

pp. 116-117

Many interesting studies of the relations between a trade union and its members have been made. Among those that are relevant to the discussion in this chapter are Gullvåg et.al. (1952 and 1953), Lysgaard (1961), Seidman et.al. (1958) and Lindblad (1960).

Among those who have studied changes in the goals and programs of trade unions are: Hart (1949) and Lipset, Trow & Coleman (1956).

Blau & Scott (1962) suggest that the more success an organization achieves, the more likely it is to seek new goals to broaden its program and ensure its continued existence.

p. 119

The reformulation of the goals of industrial democracy suggested here, involves an interpretation of the generally accepted goals and evaluations of a democracy. However, it must be pointed out that other goals have been suggested by other writers. For some socialist theorists, the ultimate goal is a system of representation and the abolition of leadership and status differential. The human relations movement, on the other hand, sought to create an environment which would promote the health of the individual and encourage the development of his personality.

p. 123

For a discussion of the problems of superior-subordinate communications, see Newcomb (1947), Carlson, Höglund & Söderman (1952), Blau & Scott (1962) and others.

p. 125

For a discussion of tough situations and complex demands as a spur to managerial efficiency, see Melman (1958) and Cyert & March (1963).

Galbraith (1952) criticizes the American building industry as a case of over-powerful trade unions, who can promote their own interests to the detriment of other stakeholders, in particular the customers. Sills (1961) cites other cases in which one stakeholder wields so much power that the others cannot uphold their interests and survival is in jeopardy.

Some interesting experiences of representation on the board have recently been published. In the main they confirm the theses put forward in the present work. Thorsrud & Emery (1963) provide a résumé and present the results of a Norwegian study of their own.

p. 131

Interesting problems of industrial democracy will be found in companies dominated by experts. The large research organizations provide a case in point and one which has been the subject of much attention. For a discussion of some of the solutions suggested – for instance "double ways up" – see Shepard (1958) or Leamer (1959).

p. 136
The satirical description of a board meeting in Parkinson (1957) reflects the attitude of many a company president to his board. At the meeting described, investment in an atomic reactor and in a bicycle stand were two of the subjects to be discussed. The board members were ignorant about the first of these and a decision could be reached in 2 1/2 minutes. On the second matter, however, every member had something to say and the debate lasted for an hour.

For a discussion of differentiated management, see Leavitt (1962a and 1962b). The difference between the situation of the management committees and work opportunities in different companies was clearly brought out by Carlson, Höglund & Söderman (1952). Cf. the references in chapter 7 to the special problems of research organizations. National variations are discussed by Clegg (1960).

p. 139
Classical studies in industrial sociology are limited not only to the USA but even to a few companies there, e.g. Western Electric (Hawthorne), Prudential Life, Detroit Edison, Baltimore & Ohio Railroad and International Harvester. To these must be added Glacier Metal in England.

Fagersta Järnverk is one of the first Swedish companies that has experimented systematically with the total socio-technical environment within a production unit.

INDEX OF SUBJECTS

LITERATURE

ACKOFF, R.L., Automatic management: A forecast and its educational implications Management science 2 (1955) 1, p. 55 ff.

ACKOFF, R.L., A definitional note on cooperation, conflict and competition. Erhvervsøkonomisk tidsskrift 26 (1962) 4, p. 312 ff.

AHLMANN, H. & RHENMAN, E., Rationaliseringsarbetets organisation och administration. Rationaliseringstekniska institutet Stockholm 1964. (Stencil.)

ANSHEN, M., The manager and the black box. Harvard business review 38 (1960) 6, p. 85 ff.

ARGYRIS, C., Understanding organizational behavior. Homewood, Ill. 1960.

BALDAMUS, W., Efficiency and effort. An analysis of industrial administration. London 1961.

BALES, R.F. & SLATER, P.E., Role differentiation in small decision making groups. PARSONS, T. & BALES, R.F. (ed.), Family. Socialization and interaction process. Glencoe, Ill. 1955.

BARNARD, C.I., The functions of the executive. Cambridge, Mass. 1938.

BARNARD, C.I., The functions and pathology of status systems in formal organizations. WHYTE, W.F. (ed.), Industry and society. New York 1946.

BARNARD, C.I., Elementary conditions of business morals. California management review 1 (1958) 1, p. 1 ff.

BASS, B.M., Leadership, psychology and organizational behavior. New York 1960.

BAUMOL, W., Business behavior value and growth. New York 1959.

BELL, D., Exploring factory life. Commentary (1947) January, p. 79 ff. MILLER, D.C. & FORM, W.H., Industrial sociology, s. 78 ff. New York 1951.

BENDIX, R., Work and authority in industry. New York 1956.

BENDIX, R. & FISHER, L.H., The perspectives of Elton Mayo. ETZIONI, A. (ed.), Complex organization: A sociological reader. New York 1961.

BENNE, K.D. & SHEATS, P., Functional roles of group members. Journal of social issues 4 (1948) 2, p. 41 ff.

BENNIS, W.G., Leadership theory and administrative behavior: The problem of authority. Administrative science quarterly 4 (1959) 3.

BERLE, A.A., Power without property. London 1960.

BLAU, P.M., The dynamics of bureaucracy. Chicago 1955.

BLAU, P.M. & SCOTT, W.R., Formal organizations. San Francisco 1962.

BLUMER, H., Social structure and power conflict. KORNHAUSER, A., DUBIN, R. & ROSS, A.M., Industrial conflict. New York 1954.
BOS, M.C., Experimental study of productive collaboration. Acta physiologica 3 (1937), p. 315 ff.
BOULDING, K.E., The organizational revolution. New York 1954.
BOULDING, K.E., Conflict and defense: A general theory. New York 1962.
BOULDING, K.E., The future corporations and public attitudes. RILEY, J.W., JR. (ed.), The corporation and its publics. New York 1963.
BRADY, R.A., Business as a system of power. New York 1943.
BRAYFIELD, A.H. & CROCKETT, W.H., Employee attitudes and employee performance. Psychological bulletin 52 (1955) 5, p. 396 ff.
BROSS, I.D.J., Design for decision. New York 1953.
BROWALDH, T., Företagaren och samhället. Ekonomisk-politiska uppsatser. Stockholm 1961.
BROWN, W., Exploration in management. London 1960.
BURNS, T. & STALKER, G.M., The management of innovation. London 1961.
CARLBERG, B.C., Företagsledaren – impulsgivaren. Stockholm 1961.
CARLSON, S., Executive behavior. Stockholm 1951.
CARLSON, S., HÖGLUND, R. & SÖDERMAN, O., Företagsnämndernas arbete, arbetssätt och effektivitet i svensk industri. Företagsekonomiska forskningsinstitutet. Stockholm 1952. (Stencil.)
CHAMBERLAIN, N.W., The firm: Micro-economic planning and action. New York 1962.
CLEGG, H.A., New approach to industrial democracy. Oxford 1960.
COCH, L. & FRENCH, J.R.P., JR., Overcoming resistance to change. Human relations 1 (1948) 4, p. 512 ff.
COMREY, A.L., PFIFFNER, J.M. & HIGH, W.S., Factors influencing organizational effectiveness. University of Southern California. Final technical report. The office of naval research. Los Angeles 1954.
CORDINER, R.J., New frontiers for professional managers. New York 1956.
COSER, R.L., The functions of social conflict. London 1956.
COSER, R.L., Authority and decision-making in a hospital: A comparative analysis. American sociological review 23 (1958) 1, p. 56 ff.
CROZIER, M., The French bureaucratic system. Stanford 1963. BLAU, P.M. & SCOTT, W.R., Formal organizations. (p. 175.) San Francisco 1962.
CYERT, R.M. & MARCH, J.G., A behavioral theory of organizational objectives. HAIRE, M. (ed.), Modern organization theory. New York 1959.
CYERT, R.M. & MARCH, J.G., A behavioral theory of the firm. Englewood Cliffs, N.J. 1963.
CYERT, R.M., SIMON, H.A. & TROW, D.B., Observation of a business decision. The journal of business 29 (1956) 4, p. 237 ff.
DAHL, R.A. & LINDBLOM, C.E., Politics, economics and welfare. New York 1953.
DAHLSTRÖM, E., Information på arbetsplatsen. Stockholm 1956.
DALE, E., Greater productivity through labour-management cooperation. American management association research report no. 14. New York 1949.
DALE, E., Planning and developing the company organization structure. New York 1952.

DALTON, M., Men who manage. New York 1959.
DAVIS, L.E., Toward a theory of job design. Journal of industrial engineering 8 (1957), p. 305 ff.
DAVIS, L.E. & CANTER, R.R., Job design. Journal of industrial engineering 6 (1955) 3.
DEARBORN, D.C. & SIMON, H.A., Selective perception: A note on the departmental identifications of executives. Sociometry 21 (1958) 2, p. 140 ff.
DEUTSCH, M., A theory of cooperation and competition. Human relations 2 (1949) 2, p. 129 ff.
DIMOCK, M.E., Administrative vitality. London 1960.
DONALDSON, G., Financial goals: Management vs. stockholders. Harvard business review 1963, May/June, s. 116 ff.
DRUCKER, P., Concept of the corporation. New York 1946.
DRUCKER, P., The new society. New York 1950.
DRUCKER, P., The practice of management. New York 1954.
DUBIN, R., Society and Union-management relations. ETZIONI, A. (ed.), Complex organizations. A sociological reader. New York 1961.
DURKHEIM, E., De la division du travail social. Paris 1932.
EDWARDS, W., The theory of decision making. Psychological bulletin 5 (1954) 4, p. 380 ff.
EDWARDS, W., Behavioral decision theory. Annual review of psychology 12 (1961), p. 473 ff.
ERICSSON, T., Skriftliga riktlinjer för företagspolitik. Affärsekonomi 6 (1960) 2, p. 811 ff.
ETZIONI, A., A comparative analysis of complex organizations. Glencoe, Ill. 1961.
FAYOL, H., Administration industrielle et générale. Paris 1965.
FIEDLER, F.E., A note on leadership theory: The effect of social barriers between leaders and followers. Sociometry 20 (1957) 2, p. 87 ff.
FLEISHMAN, E.A., HARRIS, E.F. & BURTT, H.E., Leadership and supervision in industry. Columbus, Ohio 1955.
FOLLET, MARY PARKER, The process of control. GULICK, L. & URWICK, L. (ed.), Papers on the science of administration. New York 1937.
FOULKES, S.H. & ANTHONY, E.J., Group psychotherapy. London 1957.
FRENCKNER, T.P., Syfta företagen mot högsta möjliga vinst? Företagsekonomiska forskningsinstitutet. Stockholm 1953.
FÜRSTENBERG, F., Probleme der Lohnstruktur. Tübingen 1958.
FÄLTSTRÖM, E. & SPARR, J., Skriftlig organisationspolitik. Stockholm 1959.
GALBRAITH, J.K., American capitalism. The concept of countervailing power. Cambridge, Mass. 1952.
GANTT, H.L., Industrial leadership. New Haven, Conn. 1916.
GILBRETH, F.B. & GILBRETH, LILIAN E., Fatigue study. London 1918.
GIRDLER, T., Boot straps. New York 1943.
GOULDNER, A.W., Patterns of industrial bureaucracy. Glencoe, Ill. 1954.
GRANICK, D., The red executive. The study of organization man in Russian industry. New York 1960.
GRANICK, D., The European executive. London 1962.
GROSS, N., MASON, W.S. & MCEACHERN, A.W., Explorations in role analysis: Studies of the school superintendency role. New York 1958.

GULICK, L. H. & URWICK, L. (ed.), Papers on the science of administration. New York 1937.
GULLVÅG, HARRIET *et al.*, Attitudes and perceptions of representatives and representees in industry. Oslo 1952 and 1953.
GÖRANSSON, K. F., Samförstånd mellan företagare och arbetare. Handel och industri. Stockholm 1927.
HANSSON, R., Gruppstruktur och produktivitet. PA-rådets meddelande nr 28. Stockholm 1962.
HARSANYI, J. C., Approaches to the bargaining problem before and after the theory of games: A critical discussion of Zeuthen's, Hicks', and Nash's theories. Econometrica 24 (1956) 2, p. 144 ff.
HART, C. W. M., Industrial relations research and social theory. Canadian journal of economics and political science 15 (1949), p. 53 ff.
HAYAKAWA, S. I., Language in thought and action, London 1952.
HEDBERG, M., Företagets personalomsättning. Personaladministrativa rådet. Stockholm 1963.
HEMPHILL, J. K., Situational factors in leadership. Leadership studies no. 4. The Ohio State University. Columbia, Ohio 1949.
HERZBERG, F., MAUSNER, B. & SNYDERMAN, BARBARA B., The motivation to work. New York 1959.
HOLDEN, P. E., FISH, L. S. & SMITH, H. L., Top management organization and control. Stanford University. Stanford, Calif. 1941.
HOMANS, G. C., Fatigue of workers. New York 1941.
HOMANS, G. C., Social behavior. Its elementary forms. London 1961.
HOPKINS, T. K., Bureaucratic authority: The convergence of Weber and Barnard. ETZIONI, A. (ed.), Complex organizations. A sociological reader. New York 1961.
HÄRNQVIST, K., Adjustment, leadership and group relations in a military training situation. Stockholm 1956.
HÖGLUND, R., Företaget i samhället. – En studie i fem industriföretags relationer med yttervärlden. Företagsekonomiska forskningsinstitutets meddelande nr 46. Stockholm 1953.
JANOWITZ, M., Professional soldier: A social and political portrait. Glencoe, Ill. 1960.
JAQUES, E., Changing culture of a factory. Tavistock, London 1951.
JENKINS, W. O., A review of leadership studies with particular reference to military problems. Psychological bulletin 44 (1947) 1, p. 54 ff.
JENNINGS, E. E., The democratic and authoritarian approaches: A comparative survey of research findings. American management association. General management report 16 (1958).
JOHNSON, H. M., Sociology – a systematic introduction. New York 1960.
KAHN, R. L. & KATZ, D., Leadership, practices in relation to productivity and morale. CARTWRIGHT, D. & ZANDER, A. (ed.), Group dynamics. Evanston, Ill. 1953.
KATONA, G., Psychological analysis of economic behavior. New York 1951.
KATZ, D. & KAHN, R. L., Human organization and worker motivation. TRIPP, L. R. (ed.), Industrial productivity. Industrial relations research association. Madison, Wisc. 1951.

KATZ, D. & KAHN, R.L., Some recent findings in human-relations research in industry. SWANSON, G.E., NEWCOMB, T.M. & HARTLEY, E.L. (ed.), Readings in social psychology. New York 1952.

KELLEY, H.H. & THIBAUT, J.W., Experimental studies of group problem solving and process. LINDZEY, G. (ed.), Handbook of social psychology. Cambridge, Mass. 1954.

KNICKERBOCKER, I., Leadership: A conception and some implications. Journal of social issues 4 (1958) Sommer, p. 23 ff.

KNOWLES, W.H., Human relations in industry: Research and concepts. California management review 1 (1958) 1, p. 87 ff.

KOONTZ, H., The management theory jungle. Journal of the academy of management 4 (1961) 3, p. 175 ff.

KOONTZ, H. & O'DONNELL, C., Principles of management. New York 1959.

KORNHAUSER, A., DUBIN, R. & ROSS, A.M. (ed.), Industrial conflict. New York 1954.

KRELLE, W., Preistheorie. Tübingen and Zürich 1961.

KRUISINGA, H. (ed.), The balance between centralization and decentralization in managerial control. Leiden 1954.

KRUPP, S., Pattern in organizational analysis. New York 1961.

LANDSBERGER, H.A., Hawthorne revisited. New York 1958.

LANDSBERGER, H.A., The horizontal dimension in bureaucracy. Administrative science quarterly 6 (1961) 3, p. 299 ff.

LASSWELL, H.D., Decision process. Bureau of governmental research. College of business and public administration. University of Maryland. College Park, Md 1956.

LASSWELL, H.D. & KAPLAN, A., Power and society. New Haven, Conn. 1950.

LEAMER, F.D., Professional and administrative ladders: Classification in a research organization. Research management 2 (1959) 1.

LEAVITT, H.J., Unhuman organizations. Harvard business review 40 (1962 a) 4, p. 90 ff.

LEAVITT, H.J., Management according to task: Organizational differentiation. Graduate school of industrial administration. Reprint no. 99. Carnegie Institute of Technology. Pittsburgh 1962 b.

LEAVITT, H.J. & WHISLER, T.L., Management in the 1980's. Harvard business review 1958 Nov./Dec., p. 41 ff.

LEIBENSTEIN, H., Economic theory and organization analysis. New York 1960.

LEWIN, K., The dynamics of group action. Educational leadership (1944) 1, p. 195 ff.

LEWIN, K., Resolving social conflicts. New York 1948.

LEWIN, K., LIPPITT, R. & WHITE, R.K., Patterns of aggressive behavior in experimentally created social climates. Journal of social psychology 10 (1939) 2, p. 271 ff.

LEWIN, K. *et al.*, Level of aspiration. HUNT, J.MCV. (ed.), Personality and the behavior disorders. New York 1944.

LEYS, W.A.R., The value framework of decision-making. MAILICK, S. & VAN NESS, E.H. (ed.), Concepts and issues in administrative behavior. Englewood Cliffs, N.J. 1962.

LIKERT, R., A motivational approach to modified theory of organizational and management theory. HAIRE, M. (ed.), Modern organization theory. New York 1959.

LIKERT, R., New patterns of management. New York 1961.
LINCOLN, J.E., Lincoln's incentive system. New York 1946.
LINCOLN, J.E., Incentive management. Cleveland, Ohio 1951.
LINDBLAD, I., Svenska kommunalarbetareförbundet 1910-1960. Stockholm 1960.
LIPSET, S.M., TROW, M.A. & COLEMAN, J.S., Union democracy. Glencoe, Ill. 1956.
LYSGAARD, S., Arbeiderkollektivet – en studie i de underordnades sosiologi. Oslo 1961.
MacKENZIE, W.J.M., Science in the study of administration. The Manchester school of economics and social studies (1952) 20, p. 1 ff.
MAIER, N.R.F., Psychology in industry. Boston 1955.
MANN, F.C. & HOFFMAN, R.L., Automation and the worker: A study of social change in power plants. New York 1960.
MANN, F.C. & WILLIAMS, L.K., Observations on the dynamics of a change to electronic data-processing equipment. Administrative science quarterly 5 (1960) 2, p. 217 ff.
MARCH, J.G. & SIMON, H.A., Organizations. New York 1958.
MARPLES, D.L., Conflict in organization. Dept. of Engineering, University of Cambridge. Cambridge 1960. (unpublished)
MASLOW, A.H., Motivation and personality. New York 1954.
MASON, E.S., The corporation in modern society. Cambridge, Mass. 1960.
MAYO, E., The social problems of an industrial civilization. Boston 1945.
McCURDY, H.G. & LAMBERT, W.E., The efficiency of small human groups in the solution of problems requiring genuine cooperation. Journal of personality 20 (1951/52), p. 478 ff.
McGREGOR, D., The human side of enterprise. New York 1960.
McGREGOR, D., On leadership. Antioch notes 31 (1954). Reference in: BENNIS, W.G., Leadership theory and administrative behavior: The problem of authority. Administrative science quarterly 4 (1959) 3, p. 260 ff.
McMURRY, R.N., The case for benevolent autocracy. Harvard business review 36 (1958) 1, p. 82 ff.
MELMAN, S., Decision-making and productivity. Oxford 1958.
MENNINGER, K., Man against himself. New York 1938.
MERTON, R.K., Social theory and social structure. Glencoe, Ill. 1957.
METCALF, H.C. & URWICK, L., Dynamic administration. London 1941.
MILLER, D.C. & FORM, W.H., Industrial sociology. New York 1951.
MILLER, W.B., Two concepts of authority. THOMPSON, J.D., Comparative studies in administration. Pittsburgh 1959.
MOONEY, J.D., The principles of organization. New York 1947.
MORENO, J.L., Who shall survive? New York, 1934.
MORSE, NANCY & REIMER, E., The experimental change of a major organizational variable. Journal of abnormal and social psychology 52 (1956), p. 120 ff.
MOSSIN, A.C., Selling performance and contentment in relation to school background. New York 1949.
NEUMANN, J. von & MORGENSTERN, O., Theory of games and economic behavior. Princeton N. J. 1947.
NEWCOMB, T.M., Autistic hostility and social reality. Human relations 1 (1947) 1, p. 69 ff.
NEWMAN, J., Co-responsibility in industry. Dublin 1955.

NEWMAN, W.H., Administrative action. New York 1951.
PARKINSON, C., N., Parkinson's Law. Boston 1957.
PARSONS, T., Suggestions for a sociological approach to the theory of organizations. Administrative science quarterly 1 (1956) 1, p. 63 ff. and 1 (1956) 2, p. 225 ff.
PARSONS, T., General theory in sociology. [Ingår i] MERTON, R.K., BROOM, L. & COTTRELL, L.S., Jr. (ed.), Sociology today. New York 1958.
PELZ, D.C., Influence: A key to effective leadership in the first-line supervisor. Personnel 29 (1952) 3, p. 209 ff.
PFIFFNER, J.M., The effective supervisor. An organization research study. Personnel 31 (1955), p. 530 ff.
PRESTHUS, R.V., Toward a theory of organizational behavior. Administrative science quarterly 3 (1958) 1, p. 48 ff.
RAMSTÉN, N. Bör de anställda ha inflytande på företagspolitiken? Affärsekonomi (1963) 10, p. 732.
RAPOPORT, A., Fights, games and debates. Ann Arbor, Mich. 1961.
RENOLD, C.G., Joint consultation over 30 years. A case study. London 1950.
RHENMAN, E., The organization – a controlled system. Stockholm 1966.
RHENMAN, E., Research planning – a complex problem. Proceedings 3rd international conference on operations research. (To be published, Paris 1964 a.)
RHENMAN, E., Organisationens mål. Sociologisk tidskrift (1964 b) 2. (To be published in English in Acta Sociologica, 1967.)
RHENMAN, E., STRÖMBERG, L. & WESTERLUND, G., Om linje och stab. En studie av konflikt och samverkan i företagets organisation. Stockholm 1963.
RHENMAN, E. & SVENSSON, S., Research administration. A selected and annotated bibliography of recent literature. AB Atomenergi, AE 28. Stockholm 1961.
RICE, A.K., Productivity and social organization. The Ahmedabad experiment. Tavistock, London 1958.
RICHARDSON, F.L. & WALKER, C.R., Human relations in an expanding company. New Haven, Conn. 1948.
RICHARDSON, L., Arms and insecurity. Pittsburgh 1959.
RIESMAN, D., Individualism reconsidered. Glencoe, Ill. 1954.
ROBERTS, D.R., A general theory of executive compensation, based on statistically tested propositions. Quarterly journal of economics 70 (1956) 2, p. 270 ff.
ROBERTS, D.R., Executive compensation. Glencoe, Ill. 1958.
ROETHLISBERGER, F.J. & DICKSON, W.J., Management and the worker. Cambridge, Mass. 1939.
RUIST, E., Industriföretagets produktionseffektivitet. Stockholm 1960.
RYAN, T.A., Work and effort. New York 1947.
SAGEN, J., Linje og stab i bedriftsorganisasjonen. Oslo 1958.
SCHELLING, T.C., Strategy of conflict. Cambridge, Mass. 1960.
SCHMIDT, W.H. & BUCHANAN, P.C., Techniques that produce teamwork. New London, 1954.
SEIDMAN, J. *et al.*, Worker views his union. Chicago 1958.
SELZNICK, P., TVA and the grass roots. Berkeley 1949.
SELZNICK, P., Leadership in administration. Evanston, Ill. 1957.

SHAW, M.E., A comparison of individuals and small groups in the rational solution of complex problems. American journal of psychology 44 (1932) 3, p. 491 ff.

SHEPARD, H.A., Superiors and subordinates in research. The journal of business 29 (1956) 4, p. 261 ff.

SHEPARD, H.A., The dual hierarchy in research. Research management 1 (1958) 3, p. 177 ff.

SHERIF, M. & SHERIF, CAROLYN W., An outline of social psychology. New York 1956.

SILLS, D.L., The succession of goals. ETZIONI, A. (ed.), Complex organizations. A sociological reader. New York 1961.

SIMON, H.A., Administrative behavior. New York 1947.

SIMON, H.A., Models of man. New York 1957 a.

SIMON, H.A., The compensation of executives. Sociometry 20 (1957 b), p. 32 ff.

SIMON, H.A., The new science of management decision. New York 1960.

SIMON, H.A., SMITHBURGH, D.W. & THOMPSON, V.A., Public administration. New York 1950.

SIMPSON, R.L., Vertical and horizontal communication in formal organizations. Administrative science quarterly 4 (1959) 2, p. 188 ff.

SLOAN, A.P., Adventures of a white-collar man. New York 1941.

SMITH, G., Parterna på arbetsmarknaden. Solna 1961.

STAGNER, R., Psychology of industrial conflict. New York 1956.

STIEGLITZ, H., Corporate organization structures. National industrial conference board. Studies in personnel policy no. 183. New York 1961.

STOGDILL, R.M., Personal factors associated with leadership: A survey of the literature. The journal of psychology 25 (1948) January, p. 35 ff.

STOGDILL, R.M., Individual behavior and group achievement. New York 1959.

STRÖMBERG, L. & WIRDENIUS, H., Beslutsprocessers uppbyggnad. Stockholm 1961.

SÖDERSTRÖM, P. & RODERT, L., Företagsnämnden. En sammanfattning efter 100 sammanträden vid AB Volvo Skövdeverken. Skövde 1962.

TAYLOR, F.W., Scientific management. New York 1947.

THOMPSON, J.D. & BATES, F.L., Technology, organization and administration. Administrative science quarterly 2 (1957) 3, p. 325 ff.

THOMPSON, J.D. & MCEWEN, W.J., Organizational goals and environment. Goalsetting as an interaction process, American sociological review 23 (1958) 1.

THOMPSON, S., Management creeds and philosophies. American management association. Research study no. 32. New York 1958.

THOMPSON, V.A., Hierarchy specialization and organizational conflict. Administrative science quarterly 5 (1961) 4.

THORNDYKE, R.L., On what type of task will a group do well? Journal of abnormal and social psychology 33 (1938), p. 409 ff.

THORSRUD, E. & EMERY, F., Industrielt demokrati – representasjon på styreplan i bedriften. Oslo 1964.

THRALL, R.M., COOMBS, C.H. & DAVIS, R.L. (ed.), Decision processes. New York 1954.

TORRANCE, E.P., Group decision-making and disagreement. Social forces 35 (1956/57) 4, p. 314 ff.

WALKER, C.R., Toward the automatic factory. New Haven, Conn. 1957.

WALKER, C.R. & GUEST, R.H., The man on the assembly line. Cambridge, Mass. 1952.

WALKER, C.R., GUEST, R.H. & TURNER, A.N., The foremen on the assembly line. Cambridge, Mass. 1956.

WALKER, C.R. & RICHARDSON, F.L.W., Human relations in an expanding company. New Haven. Conn. 1948.

WALPOLE, G.S., Management and men, London 1944.

WARNER, W.L. & MARTIN, N.H. (ed.), Industrial man. New York 1959.

WEBER, M., Theory of social and economic organization. Oxford 1947.

WESTERLUND, G., Samverkan mellan företagsledning och anställda. WESTERLUND, G. (ed.), Människan och arbetet. Stockholm 1951.

WESTERLUND, G., Behaviour in a work situation with functional supervision and with group leaders. Stockholm 1952.

WESTERLUND, G., Industripsykologen, hans måttproblem och hans föreställningsramar. Bedriftsøkonomen 20 (1958) 1, p. 131 ff.

WHYTE, W.H., JR., The organization man. New York 1956.

WIGFORSS, E., Näringslivets demokratisering - de anställda och företaget. FLYBOO, T. *et al.*, Medbestämmanderätten i företagen. Örebro 1956.

WOODWARD, JOAN, Management and technology. London 1958.

WOOTTON, BARBARA, The social foundations of wage policy. London 1955.

WÄRNERYD, K.-E., Motiv och beslut i företagsledningens marknadspolitik. Företagsekonomiska forskningsinstitutets meddelande nr 53. Stockholm 1957.

WÄRNERYD, K.-E., Ekonomisk psykologi. Stockholm 1959.

ZAAR, K., Är framtidens företagsledare en "hårding" eller "hygglig prick"? Ekonomen (1962) 13, p. 22 ff.

Arbetarrörelsens efterkrigsprogram. Stockholm 1944.

Dagens Nyheter 22 maj 1962. Nicolins parkering (tema på arbetsstudiekongress).

Den industriella demokratins problem. Stockholm 1923.

Fackföreningsrörelsen och företagsdemokratin. Stockholm 1961.

Journal of conflict resolution, 1 (1957) –.

Människan i arbetet. (Folkpartiet. Arbetsgrupp 2.) Stockholm 1961. (Stencil.)